Craving The Addiction

Resource Guide All Skill Levels of Barn Quilt Artists

Talara Parrish, Artist & Author

About The Author

Talara Parrish is a passionate artist and the founder of Barn Quilt Headquarters, a creative hub dedicated to the artistry of barn quilt making. Talara discovered her love for quilting and painting at a young age, and over the years, she had the opportunity to meet and motivate other aspiring artists. However, it was her deep appreciation for the enthusiasm others had for the art form and what was missing as resources for artists that truly captivated her heart.

Driven by her love for barn quilts, Talara founded Barn Quilt Headquarters to promote this unique art form and provide a platform for fellow enthusiasts to explore their creativity. Located in a picturesque rural setting of the Blue Ridge Mountains, Barn Quilt Headquarters serves as a gathering place for artists, customers, and individuals interested in learning about, creating, owning, or admiring barn quilts.

Talara's vision for Barn Quilt Headquarters goes beyond simply offering workshops and events. She aims to create an immersive experience where visitors can learn about the history and significance of barn quilts while keeping the tradition alive through their own creations.

The headquarters is adorned with Talara's own stunning barn quilt designs, showcasing her talent and passion for the art. Talara has collaborated with local craftsmen to ensure that the headquarters exudes a warm, welcoming atmosphere that mirrors the charm of the surrounding mountain views.

Through Barn Quilt Headquarters, visitors can participate in workshops where Talara guides them through the process of designing and painting their own barn quilts. These workshops cater to all skill levels, ensuring that beginners and experienced painters alike can find inspiration and expand their knowledge.

In addition to workshops, Barn Quilt Headquarters encourages exhibitions, artists gatherings, and community events centered around barn quilts. Talara firmly believes that barn quilts connect people and communities, and she encourages local artists to showcase their work, fostering a sense of unity and collaboration.

Through Barn Quilt Headquarters, Talara is dedicated to preserving the rich tradition of barn quilts while encouraging creativity and artistic expression. Her love for this unique art form shines through in every aspect of the headquarters, making it a must-visit destination for all those fascinated by the beauty and barn quilt designs.

Let's give credit to AI, because I am not that smart in talking about myself!

—

Table of Contents

To keep the page count and cost of this publication down, a choice was made not to include color inspirations for all patterns.

e

"Barn Quilts are like tattoos, you can't stop with just one." —Talana Parrish

What is this book all about?

I am excited to offer the third book in the Barn Quilt Addiction series and there are so many new patterns. I wish I had the time to paint all of these. At least doing the design work gives me a creative outlet and I enjoy that process just as much as painting. I thought about using AI but that ain't me. So here it is, grammar and spelling errors and all.

I have many more original patterns in this edition and have included circle based, point based along with the standard grid-based patterns. Whether a beginner or a thriving enthusiast, there is something for everyone.

I wanted to take the opportunity to celebrate the success of others. This gives me the most pleasure and I am honored to play a small role in some of their stories.

I have had the pleasure of personally meeting so many wonderful people. Our 1st Annual Barn Quilt Artist Retreat was held in my hometown of West Jefferson, NC. In July 2023. It was a great success, and we have about 40 attendees. I can't describe how much fun it was for us to meet each other since we have all met on social media. Putting a face and a personality with a comment or post was so much better than we imagined. I hope that this event continues for years to come, and we can hold it in other locations throughout the coming years.

As part of this event, we held the 1st National Barn Quilt Competition and Auction. We had over 40 submittals and everyone a beautiful work of art.

I have spent countless hours upon hours graphing these patterns and had to cut it off somewhere. I could have another 100 but next book maybe. I did my best to illustrate so that anyone can follow the pattern. Sometimes it is challenging to explain the more advanced ones but with a few under your belt, you should be able to accomplish those that look intimidating to draw out.

It is just all math! Should have paid attention in call instead of the cutie sitting next to you!

–

What is a Barn Quilt?

A barn quilt is a large, decorative piece of artwork that is displayed on the exterior of a building, typically a barn. It is inspired by traditional quilt patterns.

What is NOT a barn quilt?

Cut wooden shapes and placed together to form a quilt pattern. This is considered "Pieced Wooden Quilt Block Art". It is not assembled or made to withstand the elements to be hung outdoors.

Canvas paintings of quilt blocks. This is also not considered a barn quilt. Why? Can you hang this outdoors in the elements? Usually not and this is considered Quilt Block Art.

Coasters, serving trays, furniture, saw blades and other items that are used to paint quilt patterns on are not barn quilts either. These also are considered Quilt Block Art.

That does not mean these are not beautiful and painted by very talented artists. However, barn quilt artists are highly offended by social media posts in barn quilt groups of these items. I guess you are wondering why. We have a hard enough time explaining what barn quilts are and developing our art form exposure. These other mediums only confuse the public.

In summary, a barn quilt is a painted quilt block (or series of) on a surface suitable for outdoor exposure whether used as exterior or interior art. The minimum size is 1' x 1'. This size is often used as a mailbox hanger.

Pattern Rule: If you can't sit at a sewing machine and make it out of fabric, it is not a barn quilt pattern.

—

Let's Brag on The Winner!

Deanna's Delightful Barn Quilt Designs is a thriving business founded by the talented artist Deanna Shuman. With a deep passion for barn quilts and a love for creativity, Deanna has established herself as a Master Barn Quilt artist and crafting stunning barn quilt patterns.

Deanna's journey into the world of barn quilt designs began when she stumbled upon an old, weathered barn showcasing an enchanting quilt pattern. This sight ignited her passion and she immediately delved into learning about the history and techniques of barn quilts. Deanna is also one of the first artists to join Barn Quilt Headquarters and she has painted many beautiful custom barn quilts for customers as orders through the site.

Deanna's barn quilt designs are characterized by their intricate details, balanced color schemes, and harmonious compositions. Each design is carefully thought out and meticulously hand-painted, ensuring that every piece she creates is a work of art.

Her talents are celebrated in her Lone Star barn quilt that won the first National Barn Quit Competition and Auction held in July 2023. Her beautiful colors made this a stunner and raised $1,163.00 in donations for the Lost Province Cultural Arts Center in Lansing, NC. This was a locally sponsored competition where the public donations and bids on their favorite out of 40 entries from various artists across the country. Not only am I proud to feature this on the cover, but she also took home a nice little check of $500 as sponsorship from 3rd/5th Bank, the corporate sponsor of the event. We raised over $6,000 total for the nonprofit.

Beyond her barn quilt designs, Deanna also offers workshops and classes where she shares her knowledge and passion with others who share her love for barn quilts. Through these educational endeavors, Deanna inspires budding artists to explore their creativity and cultivate a deeper appreciation for the art of barn quilt making.

Deanna's Delightful Barn Quilt Designs has garnered a loyal following of admirers who appreciate her impeccable craftsmanship and eye-catching designs. Whether it is a traditional quilt pattern, a custom design, or a contemporary interpretation, Deanna's barn quilt creations never fail to captivate and delight.

Congratulations Deanna!

–

Our Other Recognized Top Placements

2nd Place
Carla Taylor
Farmer's Star

3rd Place
Julie Elder
Thistle Rose

4th Place
Carol Mitchell
Montjoy

5th Place
Ashley Cone
Peaceful

In Their Own Words

I also want to share some stories from other artists and how the therapy of painting barn quilts has impacted their lives.

Julie Glover – My Addiction

I belong to a group of community volunteers who joined together to help revitalize the historic downtown area in our rural Delta town of about 4,100. We began by painting a mural of sunflowers on the side of a building, then we painted the Victorian gazebo on the square with a five-color pallet to accentuate the beautiful trim. We received many accolades for all the hours we spent painting. Passersby would stop and chat, some even joined our group. The sanitation crew would applaud and shout words of encouragement as they passed by daily, several residents added us to their daily walking routes. We felt that we were accomplishing our goal of beautifying our community while participating in the fun activity of painting. There were other benefits to these projects. We enjoyed our time together, the physical exercise involved in painting on scaffolding and ladders, as well as the challenges of weather-related issues. During our discussions of future projects, we noted that the projects we had done could be viewed by much of the community. Even those with limited mobility could see and enjoy these projects, if their friends or family could take them in a car for an afternoon ride through town. But what about the older residents of our community who have lost their mobility and have the need for nursing assistance in their daily lives? We have a wonderful care facility where many older residents live, but they are confined, due to their health issues. Some of our group have family members there and felt there surely could be a way for us to bring some sunshine to their days, as well. One of the members of our group saw a post on your Facebook page showing several Barn Quilts attached to a wooden fence! That was our answer!!! It took our group two months to research, plan, organize, graph, and paint 17 4'x4' quilt blocks. Some were painted by a local women's group at the Methodist church, some by families of the residents at the nursing home, and some by individuals who just love to paint. Our largest group was 25 who worked one Saturday to complete the last six. The volunteers ranged in age from 9 to 80! That was a very special event. The completed blocks were installed on the wooden fence facing the dining halls of the nursing home just before Thanksgiving. Many new friendships were made, community pride grew, and we feel we are honoring the residents by spreading a little sunshine in their lives...even on cloudy days. ♥ *We are grateful for the information and inspiration we received from you and your followers which enabled us to complete this project.*

Painted Ladies-Marianna, AR

–

Mary E Smith

My name is Mary E. Smith from Newfield, NY. I am so happy to be able to tell you why I love Barn Quilts!

They help tell the story of "life on our farm."

Mike and I have worked together on our small farm in central NY for nearly 50 yrs.

It became our hobby to do it together! We raised crops, beefers, and many pigs, along with two children. Mike worked as a dairy cow breeder and tractor salesman for many years.

Mike became ill with Alzheimer's and during the years that the disease progressed we started traveling on "Barn Quilt Trails"!! He loved it so much! Thus started my desire to paint them. So, after my dear hubby passed on to heaven, I started painting.

I have been a quilter for many years, thus becoming familiar with many of the different quilt blocks.

The family barn, a 200-year-old one burned to the ground in early spring of 2022, and we lost some precious piglets and mama pig, as well as many precious memories! It was very sad, but my son is rebuilding and wants a barn quilt for the new barn!! YEA!

So far, I have sold only two: a 1' x 1' with the cardinal, and a 2' x 2' Lemoyne star. I would love to paint and sell more but can't figure out how that's done yet!

Thanks so much Talara for the great books, your blog where you share your talent and for the help you are so willing to give to us beginners out here!!

May God Bless,

Mary

Janet Riggs but my family calls me "Janny"

Floyds Knobs, IN (Yes it really is a place! Some people call it "Snobs Knobs" but there are a lot of nice people here.)

I have sewed almost my entire life; thankful my mom taught me how. About 10 yrs. ago my girlfriends got me started on Quilting and I started going to quilt conventions and shows with them. They are retired and I wasn't at the time, so I started gathering stuff so I would have supplies when I retire. One of the quilting groups I belong started posting barn quilt pictures and I thought those are cool. So, I searched for somewhere to take classes and dragged my friends to a class in Tenn. Just one time and I was hooked. I am the painter in our house and love to paint so it clicked with me. So, I found some supplies and painted me another one to put next to my front door, using the same colors as the door. The more I talked about it, the more my friends and family got interested. When I went on vacation, my sister wanted me to bring my stuff so she could paint one. Then my dog sitter, and my garbage man and the list go on. It has taken the place of fabric quilting for a while, but I left my box of barn supplies with my friends, so I had to go back to fabric quilting for a while! LOL I'm happy to report that I am retired now, so have more time to be artistic. My computer is filled with pictures of both barn quilts and fabric quilts. I am very thankful for Talara sharing her skills as it has taught me so much. It truly is an addiction.

I can't express how deeply I am touched by the letters and emails that I receive. I appreciate the compliments, but the bigger joy is knowing that others are enjoying the art form as much I am influencing them. Each one is precious to me and gives me motivation to keep doing what I do, no matter how long the days and nights are, how many emails, texts, and messages I get. Customer orders are great, and I enjoy those too but passing along a customer to another artist is a bigger thrill!

All this and more are why I dedicate so much time to making sure every request is taken care of and as economically as possible. The blog is a tool that allows me to be myself and give verbal instructions and information that can not be translated thoroughly in a brief post or written words.

If you are not a current member of the blog on the website, you are missing out. You may know everything about painting a barn quilt from beginning to end but never as entertained as these videos can be. I am myself, no make-up, maybe in my pj's and hair every which way possible on my head. I don't pretend to be something I am not and if the mood hits or the opportunity presents itself, phone, camera, action! Laugh with me or at me, it doesn't matter if we are both enjoying ourselves.

Craft Fairs, Markets and Quilt Shows

I am not going to be someone that recommends working and preparing pre-made barn quilts for any of these venues. 9 times out of 10 you will put hours and money into having so many barn quilts ready for these and be disappointed.

You will labor to pack up all your inventory, travel to a venue, pay for space rental, unpack, set up, arrange, find damage to a few in transporting, and spend all day either sweating in the hot sun or freezing on a chilly fall day. If you are lucky, it will be an indoor venue that undoubtedly your space is so far away from the door and before the first potential customer walks by, you are exhausted and over it.   Just wait, it gets better.

You spend all day, usually trying to handle the booth alone, talking to curious on lookers and explaining over and over what a barn quilt is, all why the potentially serious one walked away. Pitching where it could be hung, justifying why this cost so much and hearing, if it was in these colors, or I need this size. And to finally ditch your spirits to the lowest you thought these could get, here is Betty Sue "oh I can paint those" or "my friend paints those all the time". Discouraging and you just are going to want to say, "bite me"! Now – time to pack it all up and go home.

Have you been there and done that? We all have. There is a way to attend these

events, but the approach should be a little different. Concentrate of a few various sizes, different patterns, and color inspirations. I have found that a dozen is a perfect amount to have. People are not overwhelmed with so many displayed and they will take time to ask more about what these are.

Promote special orders, be sure to have something to show patterns. These books are fantastic for that. Have pictures and banners of how these can be used for curb appeal on a home, not just art for a barn. Always have an additional person on hand that is a conversationalist. I take my mom; she will talk to anyone. This helps me to be available to discuss special orders and how that process works. Of course, if someone wants to buy one, whip out that credit card! Be sure you can accept cards because most people do not come prepared with that much cash. They will not be able to use the excuse, "I don't have cash".

Also, the number one marketing material that you can have is a rack card. I don't waste my money on business cards. Those get tossed and have limited information. Rack cards provide more and can really have a visual impact that will stimulate interest once the potential customer is out of site.

Don't stress it if you don't sell that many the day of the show or get special order commitments. Those will come. I usually end up with no less than 15 orders per every 100 people that inquire the day of the show. I also offer a discount at the show so I can track business that comes from it. Here again, rack cards are great to put this discount on.

If you teach classes, also have handouts for those that express an interest in making their own. I give an overview of what materials cost to make just one and compare it to doing a class where everything is provided. Have a sign-up sheet for those interested so you can email them with information on any upcoming classes. They won't remember you; you must remember them.

I also have an informative handout on what a barn quilt is. This just helps to educate interested parties and they can read later, hopefully motivating them to spot a place they can proudly hang one. I do emphasize that barn quilts are no longer for barns and the most popular place trending in this growing art form is on homes, fences, and business.

Colors & Working with Customers

When it comes to choosing paint colors that go well together for a barn quilt, there are several key factors to consider:

What color is the surface it will be hanging on. What colors are going to be around it such as house color trim, flowers that bloom nearby, cushions on porch furniture. Complementing or mirroring these colors can create a cohesive and harmonious look and make the barn quilt truly stand out.

What colors does the customer gravitate to such as earth tones, jewel tones, pastels, neon's, vibrant or muted tones. This can give a feel for what will appeal to the customer. I always asked what their favorite color is and that gives me an idea of where to begin.

Here is a tip that I find works for me. I never lay my paint chips out where the customer can gravel through those. I pull colors as I ask questions. This helps to keep the customer focused and eliminates overwhelming them in the decision-making process. Once I have a direction and a few colors in mind, I lay the paint chips against a white surface. If they don't like the color I pull, I put it back and choose another.

Using this process, I can quickly narrow down the colors that makes the customer feel in control and comfortable deciding. I do this process prior to showing any colors laid out digitally on the computer.

Here is another valuable tip. If the customer asked for a picture of the final choice, try not to give this to them. Why? Here is what I explain to them. "If I you take this and hang on the frig, by the time I paint it, you are going to second guess your choice." Most agree to wait for the phone call when it is ready!

Using The Color Wheel -

Understanding the color wheel can help in selecting paint colors that harmonize. The color wheel consists of primary colors (red, blue, yellow), secondary colors (orange, green, purple), and tertiary colors (combination of primary and secondary colors). Colors opposite each other on the color wheel are complementary and tend to create a vibrant contrast when used together.

Color Harmony: Different color harmonies can be achieved by selecting colors strategically. Some popular color harmony schemes include:

Selecting colors that are adjacent to each other on the color wheel, such as blue, blue-green, and green.

Monochromatic: Choosing different shades, tints, and tones of a single color.

Triadic: Combining three colors that are evenly spaced on the color wheel, like red, yellow, and blue.

Mood and Atmosphere: Consider the desired mood or atmosphere of placement. Warmer colors like reds, oranges, and yellows evoke energy and vibrancy, while cooler colors like blues and greens create a sense of calmness and serenity.

Keep in mind the lighting and distance a barn quilt will be viewed from. Does it need an unexpected pop of color to draw attention to it? Colors may appear different when used next to each other. For instance, my hunter green looks like Christmas year-round when used against a red so I avoid placing the two together. Unless they want a Christmas themed barn quilt.

Contrast and Balance: Achieving a balance between colors that provide contrast and those that work harmoniously is key. Choosing a mix of light, medium, and dark tones can create a visually appealing composition.

Remember, choosing paint colors is both a creative and subjective process. Trust your instincts and experiment. The most important thing is to select colors that make the customer satisfied and create a visually pleasing impact on their barn quilt. They are the ones that must look at it although you tried to talk them into that lavender that looked better to you.

As for me, I throw the color wheel out the window. I pull my colors from things I see around me. I may see a dress while shopping and love the colors in the print. I snap a picture and put together another paint collection option on the website.

I have narrowed down the paint colors that I offer, and these options cover all that I have needed to date. It is rare that I don't have the shade of green or blue that the customer is attracted to. If a customer has a specific color, they want me to use, I am happy to, but I do charge an additional fee per color.

I am including these colors in here so that it may help you build your inventory. I am steadfast in my promotion of using sample paints. I am so frustrated with myself because I had the opportunity to take a picture of how much exterior paint fades in a short time.

Paints: Exterior or Interior

There was a retail store in town that got direct sunlight all day and faced west. It was painted avocado green. Shortly after being freshly painted, they hung a barn quilt. This business closed about two years later and the owner of the building took the barn quilt down. I drove by late in the evening and noticed how much that green wall had faded against the square that the barn quilt hung over. It was 10 shades lighter at least. My brief thought was, "that would be a perfect example of exterior paint's tendency to fade drastically" and I should get in picture. I was in a hurry and thought I'd come back the next day and do this.

The next day was busy, and I did not get back to town until the following day. I dashed up there to get my "proof" picture and low and behold, they had already painted the building for the new tenants. Crap, I was pissed at myself. Darn it! Can you believe that auto correct just tried to change "crap" to something less "offensive". I really wanted that other word & others!

Therefore, I use the sample paint with a sealer. I can walk out to any of my barn quilts and hold the paint chip up to it and the color is still as vibrant as the day I painted it. So, you do you! If you prefer the expense and storing quarts and gallons of exterior paint, that is a choice you must make. I for one will stick with what has proven to work for me and after 4, 058 barn quilts, I am not likely to change my opinion of my choice of paint.

I am not going into the details of products, paints, step by step and other information that would just be repetitive from the first two books. I have beat that horse until it is dead and if you have invested in this book, you are likely to already have those.

So back to colors. I love these colors and it is rare that I don't have one that a customer wants. It is important to have light and dark to contrast with a color. This helps give a three-dimensional look in some patterns or achieve that monochrome look.

These are all Valspar colors and available at Lowes.

If you use the BQ Designer program on the website, it will come with codes so that the pattern will reflect these actual paint colors. I also provide you with equivalent colors in all other popular manufactures. Check out the demo on the website under Artist Tools.

Paint Colors

White	Cuddle	Peach Tickle	Honey Glaze
Golden Promise	Pirate's Treasure	Tupelo Honey	Orange Glow
Orange Fruit	Island Orange	Sassy Peach	Orange Slice
Sandy Peppers	Terra Cotta Red	Autumn Enchantment	Steelhead Red
Sweet Rosewood	Decadent Red	Plumberry	Red Henna
Cosmic Pink	Cosmic Berry	Berry Brown	Antique Burgandy

Rosey Checks

Harmonious Rose

Berry Twist

Rose Dust

Very Berry

Perfect Pout

Jazzy Red

Red Bliss

Classic Red

Heirloom Red

Spanish Tile

Ancient Burgandy

Fresh Mint

Simply Aqua

Tantalizing Teal

Mint Gala

Sea Treasure

New Meadow

Tropical Rainforest

Green Suede

Green Surpreme

Salon Green

Ginkgo Tree

Hanging Vine

Archisa

Sunlit Meadow

Verde

New Avocado

Crushed Oregano

Boughs of Pine

Asparagus

Vintage Chartreuse

Bright Parrot

Nobel Eric

Wilderness

Organza

Sassy Violet

Simply Purple

Blue Ember

Spirit Blue

Air Kiss

Sonic Sky

Sea Frolic

Blue Burst

Bandana

Blue Biro

Deep Twilight Blue

Indigo Cloth

Enchanted Navy

Blue Coal

Perfect Storm

Beach Sparkle

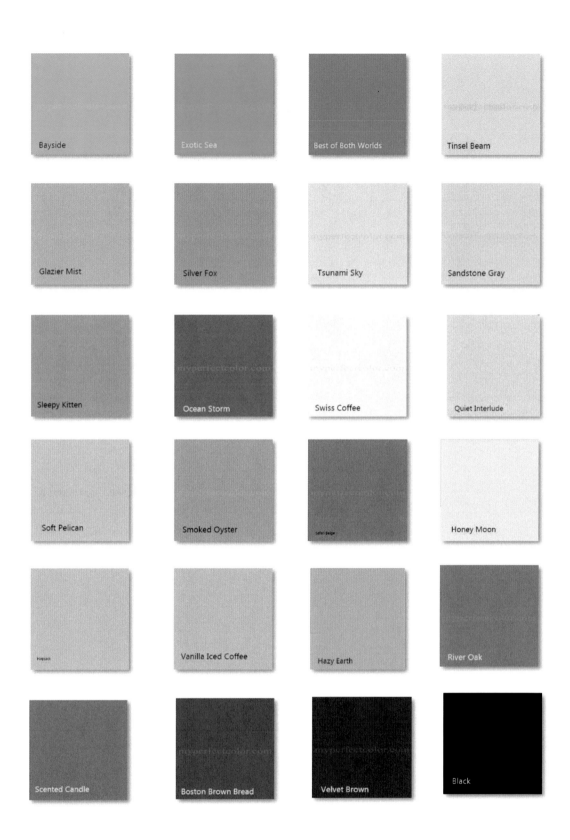

Bayside

Exotic Sea

Best of Both Worlds

Tinsel Beam

Glazier Mist

Silver Fox

Tsunami Sky

Sandstone Gray

Sleepy Kitten

Ocean Storm

Swiss Coffee

Quiet Interlude

Soft Pelican

Smoked Oyster

Safari Beige

Honey Moon

Hopsack

Vanilla Iced Coffee

Hazy Earth

River Oak

Scented Candle

Boston Brown Bread

Velvet Brown

Black

You Want to Be a therapist?

Teaching barn quilt classes can be a rewarding and fulfilling experience for both the instructor and the participant. However, like any endeavor, there are also potential pitfalls to be mindful of. Here are some rewards and pitfalls to consider:

Rewards of Teaching Barn Quilt Classes:

1. Sharing Passion and Knowledge: Teaching barn quilt classes allows you to share your passion for this unique art form and pass on your knowledge and skills to others. Inspiring and empowering participants to create their own beautiful barn quilt designs can bring immense satisfaction.

2. Building a community: Teaching barn quilt classes brings together individuals who share a common interest in art, quilting, and creativity. It provides an opportunity to create a supportive and engaging community of like-minded people who can learn from and support each other.

3. Encouraging Creativity: Barn quilt classes encourage participants to explore their creative side and express themselves through art. It can help them develop their artistic skills, fellowship, and just have fun.

4. Personal Growth: Teaching others requires effective communication, patience, and adaptability. It challenges you to continually improve your teaching methods, enhance your knowledge, and gain insights from your students. This can lead to personal satisfaction and reward of spreading the love of barn quilts.

Patience! It requires an abundance of this.

Pitfalls of Teaching Barn Quilt Classes:

1. Skill Variations: Participants in barn quilt classes may have varying levels of artistic skills, experience, and confidence. Balancing the class to accommodate individuals with different needs and providing personalized attention can be challenging.

2. Technical Instruction: Teaching the technical aspects of barn quilt making, such as measuring, marking, and painting techniques, requires clear and concise instruction. Ensuring that participants understand and apply these techniques correctly can be time-consuming and may occasionally lead to confusion or misunderstandings.

3. Time Management: Designing, creating, and completing a barn quilt can be a time-intensive process. Managing the class schedule, ensuring all participants

progress at a similar pace, and allocating enough time for each step of the process needs careful planning and organization.

4. Equipment and Supplies: Barn quilt classes require appropriate equipment and ample supplies, including MDO or aluminum composite panels, paints, brushes, measuring tools, and other materials. Ensuring that there are enough resources to accommodate all participants and maintaining their quality can be a logistical challenge.

To mitigate some of the potential pitfalls, it's important to set clear expectations, provide thorough instruction, and maintain open communication with the students. Flexibility, patience, and a nurturing teaching environment can help create a positive and enriching experience for everyone involved.

If you prepare your participants prior to the class for what to expect, and clearly outline the project, then this will be a success. I hear so many horror stories about poorly executed classes and unprepared instructors. This gives all of us a bad name and teaching should be taken seriously. No short cuts in materials, time or expense should ever be taken. Never try to offer a class inexpensively just to participate and never let anyone leave without a completed barn quilt.

Take pictures and post these on social media. Encourage participants to tag themselves and share. This spreads the word and builds interest for other and future classes.

I highly recommend that you attend a minimum of two barn quilt classes from two different *experienced* barn quilt instructors. Key to that is being experienced. You will find what works in a class and what doesn't. For your first class, do one for a few friends or family. Manage it as you would in any other class and if you must do it for free, do it. You will get honest, sometimes too honest, feedback and can test your structure and methods prior to offering classes to the public.

Pinterest, Etsy, social media & Copyrights

First, let me state clearly. I despise Pinterest and Etsy. I rarely ever visit those sites. I learned early on, never send a customer there to "find something you like". One of my customers did, found one she liked and bought it. So did twenty other people along the way. If you want to risk losing your customers, send them on. But wouldn't you rather have a collaborative design that has a little of you and your customer. Why have something that everyone else has?

I also don't sell through those sites because their fees are way too high, and shipping is a nightmare. I also prefer a personal connection with my customer.

Copyrights

Yes, quilt patterns can be copyrighted, but it's important to distinguish between copyright protection for the actual design and copyright protection for the specific instructions or printed materials for making the quilt.

The design or pattern itself, including the arrangement of *abstract* shapes, colors, and motifs, can be protected by copyright as an original artistic work. This means that reproducing, distributing, or using the design without permission from the copyright holder may infringe upon their rights.

However, copyright protection does not extend to the functional aspects of a quilt pattern, such as the *basic geometric shapes*. Copyright law typically protects the expression of an idea, not the idea itself. Therefore, creating a unique design using common geometric shapes may not qualify for copyright protection.

Confused? If the pattern is made up of triangles, squares, circles, etc. and arranged to form a pattern cannot be copyrighted. If a flower, for example, or a non-geometrical shape is incorporated into the pattern, it can be a copyrighted pattern.

Here is another example that pains me. This pattern was given the name by me of "Love's Blossom" in the Barn Quilt Addiction book. It cannot be reproduced in print and the pattern instructions sold as "Love's Blossom" by any other party. It can be reproduced as an artistic barn quilt by anyone who desires to paint it. If another person wants to market or sell this pattern in print or video, they must rename it. This is something that really upsets me when I see my named patterns instructions and transfers sold by others under the same name.

So can you produce instructions for the Weathervane pattern and sell it. Yes, because this is a common traditional quilt pattern passed down for generations. So, if you are producing videos or printed materials for any pattern, do your research and respect others. I always try but sometimes I am sent patterns to graph out and who knows who the originator is. I always rename the pattern so as not to step on toes.

It's essential to respect the copyright of quilt patterns and designs that are protected. Before using a quilt pattern, it's recommended to check if the pattern is explicitly stated as being copyrighted or if there are any usage restrictions specified by the designer or copyright holder. This can usually be found in the pattern instructions or through contact with the copyright holder.

Moreover, it's worth noting that some quilt patterns may be available for personal or non-commercial use under a Creative Commons license or similar agreements. In these cases, specific conditions regarding attribution, non-commercial use, or modifications may apply, so it's important to familiarize oneself with the terms and requirements.

If you plan to knowingly use or distribute quilt patterns commercially or in a way that might infringe on copyrights, it is advisable to seek permission from the copyright holder or consider designing your unique patterns to avoid any legal issues.

Reproducing an Inspiration

Knock yourself out with any pattern in these books. That is what the purpose is. I am always flattered when I see one of my barn quilts patterns reproduced.

The only time I become irritated is when someone takes my actual photograph of a painted barn quilt and posts it as theirs. Really? Paint your own and post that picture proudly! I spend one whole day to reported over 60 posts on Etsy of my actual photos used to promote businesses. Sad, just sad. That person has been banned from Etsy but who has time to police those sites? Not me.

You should always give recognition to another artist if you were inspired by their work. They do appreciate this, at least I do. If you resource a pattern from somewhere, such as these books, you should always give credit for this also. This allows others that may be interested in painting the same pattern on where to find it.

I have approximately 200 patterns in this book and many originals also. I have many more that I have saved in files and in my collection of old (old) quilting books and magazines. There will never be enough time to convert all to barn quilt drawing instructions.

Personally, I have a goal of a barn quilt on every home, business, or barn across the country so there is plenty of work for all of us!

Patterns

When it comes to quilt patterns, there are two common approaches: point-based patterns and grid-based patterns. Each approach has its own unique characteristics and offers different design possibilities. Here's a comparison between the two:

A grid pattern is measured out in equal divisions of the width of your board.

A point-based pattern is measured from the center out and based on degrees.

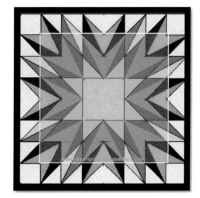

This is grid based – "Squared"

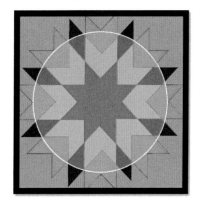

This is point based – "Round"

If any pattern which has connecting points that form a circle, cannot be broken down in a grid layout. No matter what someone tries to tell you, it will not come out with the correct angles.

To draw a point-based pattern, there is a basic rule. Every measurement is from the center out. Lateral and horizontal lines connect to those measurements.

Point based patterns are the most difficult to illustrate and are considered advance patterns. You will require going back to your geometry class that most of us never knew we'd need. I, for one, paid no attention. I sewed and was taught between your nose and fingertip held straight out measured a yard of fabric and that was good enough for me. Do have your protractor handy? And a compass too and you can achieve these.

Promoting Barn Quilts

Whether it's the process of designing and creating barn quilts or the joy of witnessing the visual transformation of buildings within a community, the barn quilt addiction has become a creative and communal way for people to engage with art and express their love for the aesthetics.

Promoting your barn quilt business can help attract customers and increase awareness about your unique offerings. Here are several strategies you can consider:

1. Establish an online presence: Create a website for your business to showcase your barn quilt designs, share the history and inspiration behind your work, and provide information on how customers can contact you or place orders. Include high-quality images, testimonials, and any relevant information that sets your business apart.

2. Utilize social media: Set up accounts on popular social media platforms like Instagram, Facebook, and Twitter. Share captivating photos of your barn quilt creations, behind-the-scenes glimpses of your creative process and engage with your audience. Consider running giveaways or contests to generate more interest and increase your online reach.

3. Collaborate with local businesses: Partner with local businesses, such as art galleries, craft stores, or home decor shops, to display or sell your barn quilts. This can help you reach a wider audience and establish connections within the community.

4. Participate in local events: Look for farmer's markets, craft fairs, festivals, or community events where you can showcase your barn quilts. Attend these events with a booth or a display to attract potential customers and network with others who appreciate art and craftsmanship. Remember to concentrate on custom orders, not moving ready-made ones.

5. Offer workshops or classes: Consider hosting workshops or classes where you teach others how to create their own barn quilts. This can generate income and raise awareness of your business.

6. Network with local organizations: Contact local historical societies, tourism bureaus, or community organizations and offer to give presentations or demonstrations about barn quilts. This can lead to collaborations or referrals.

7. Develop relationships with media outlets: Reach out to local newspapers, magazines, or television stations and share your story. Offer to provide them

with unique angles, human interest stories, or photos of your barn quilts, which can lead to coverage and exposure for your business.

Remember to always provide exceptional customer service, deliver high-quality products, and encourage satisfied customers to leave reviews or testimonials. Building a strong reputation through word of mouth can be invaluable for the growth of your barn quilt business.

Attend an Artist Retreat

A barn quilt artist retreat is a specialized retreat or workshop designed for artists interested in creating barn quilts. These retreats provide a unique opportunity for artists to delve into the world of barn quilt making, learn new techniques, enhance their skills, and connect with like-minded individuals.

Typically held in rural or scenic locations, barn quilt artist retreats offer a conducive environment for creativity and inspiration. Participants are often provided with dedicated studio spaces equipped with the necessary tools and materials to create their barn quilts. The retreats may vary in length, ranging from a few days to several weeks, allowing artists ample time to immerse themselves in their creative process.

During a barn quilt artist retreat, experienced instructors, or mentors guide participants through the various stages of barn quilt creation. They may teach traditional quilt block patterns, color theory, design principles, and techniques for painting or constructing barn quilts. Workshops may also cover topics like material resourcing & vendors, surface preparation, weatherproofing, and installation methods.

Apart from the technical aspects, these retreats also aim to foster a sense of community among participants. Artists can network, share ideas, offer feedback, and collaborate on group projects. The supportive environment allows for artistic growth and encourages participants to explore their unique artistic voices within the barn quilt medium.

Barn quilt artist retreats often incorporate other activities and experiences as well. This may include field trips to local barn quilt installations, visits to historical landmarks, recreational activities and other significant events, or guest lectures by renowned artists. These additional components enrich the overall retreat experience, offering participants a deeper appreciation for the art form and its connection to local heritage.

Attending a barn quilt artist retreat can benefit artists in various ways. They gain new skills and techniques, find inspiration from their surroundings and fellow artists, and have dedicated time and space to focus on their craft. Additionally, the retreats provide opportunities for personal growth, forging connections within the artistic community, and cultivating a renewed passion for barn quilt design and creation.

Overall, barn quilt artist retreats are exceptional opportunities for artists to expand their knowledge, refine their skills, and immerse themselves in the beauty and history of this unique art form.

I encourage anyone that wants to indulge themselves in a great time, learn and network with others and to be more motivated and empowered to take their addiction to the next level, just attend the Barn Quilt Artist Retreat. These are currently planned annually and are hosted by volunteers. We have many corporate sponsors such as Piedmont Plastics, Valspar, Lowes, and several other barn quilt businesses.

Lifetime friendships are made, and inspiration abounds!

Directory of Patterns

Beginner Patterns	BQH Original	Grid Count	Page
Bachelor's Star		5 grid	37
Boston Star		8 grid	38
Braided Ribbon		13 grid	39
Calico Star		8 grid	40
Crown Of Thorns		5 grid	41
Dutchman's Puzzle		4 grid	42
Elaine's Block		8 grid	43
Embrace		16 grid	44
Eye Catching		5 grid	45
Fancy Ribbon		8 grid	46
Flywheel		6 grid	47
Folk Art Star		6 grid	48
Folded Flag		6 grid	49
Fresca		8 grid	50
In God's Eye		8 grid	51
Carpenter's Square		6 grid	52
Mezmerized		8 grid	53
Mystery Quilt Block		8 grid	54
Paper Pinwheel	BQHO	8 grid	55
Patchwork Sunflower		8 grid	56
Patriot Sampler		24 grid	57
Peacemaker		9 grid	58
Rhododendron		6 grid	59
Ribbon		4 grid	60
Seesaw		4 grid	61
Shining Star		8 grid	62
Spools		8 grid	63
Star Within a Star		8 grid	64
Sunflower		8 grid	65
To the Point		10 grid	66
Twist & Shout		6 grid	67
Unity Star		8 grid	68
Windmill		5 grid	69
Wisconsin		5 grid	70

Directory of Patterns

Intermediate Patterns	BQH Original	Grid Count	Page
All Points		8 Grid	73
All Twisted		8 Grid	75
Appalachian Heritage	BQHO	10 Grid	77
Argyle	BQHO	11 Grid	79
Artist Block		10 Grid	81
Aspire		12 Grid	83
Astrodelic		16 Grid	85
At The Corral	BQHO	16 Grid	87
Barn Quilt Queen's Crown	BQHO	12 Grid	89
Beaming Star		8 Grid	91
Bear Cub		8 Grid	93
Bear Trap		10 Grid	95
Bee Blessing	BQHO		96
Beekeeper		7 Grid	97
Bees Knees		17 Grid	98
Bible Testiment		8 Grid	101
Boxed Double Star		8 Grid	103
Cardinal Pair		7 Grid	105
Carolina Dogwood		14 Grid	107
Colored Pencils		12 Grid	108
Corn Husk	BQHO	4 Grid	111
Cutie Patootie		8 Grid	113
Dogwood Block		8 Grid	115
Double Carpenter's Wheel		12 Grid	117
Double Rustic Star		8 Grid	119
Elegant Star		8 Grid	121
English Garden		12 Grid	123
Fall Leaves		12 Grid	124
Fall Season		16 Grid	125
Family Tree		12 Grid	126
Father's Choice		4 Grid	127
Farmer's Wife		5 Grid	129
Favored Star		8 Grid	131
Fish	BQHO	15 Grid	132
Flamboyant	BQHO	12 Grid	135
Florida Star		6 Grid	137

Directory of Patterns

Intermediate Patterns	BQH Original	Grid Count	Page
Flowering Garden		10 Grid	139
Fluttering Butterflies	BQHO	20 Grid	141
Four Leaf Glover		15 Grid	143
Four Star General		14 Grid	145
Framed Blocked Star		8 Grid	147
Full Coop		12 Grid	149
Game Night	BQHO	12 Grid	151
Go Fish	BQHO	12 Grid	133
Guardian Angel	BQHO	20 Grod	153
Happy Little Camper		8 Grid	155
Heritage	BQHO	12 Grid	157
Homestead Star	BQHO	12 Grid	159
Indian Spirit		16 Grid	161
Java Jolt	BQHO	10 Grid	163
King's Crown		8 Grid	165
Lead by Faith	BQHO	12 Grid	167
Lily		12 Grid	169
Look Here		10 Grid	171
Lotus Flower		16 Grid	173
Love Me Knot		12 Grid	175
Love Note		6 Grid	177
Loving Hearts		12 Grid	179
Magic Stars		10 Grid	181
Merry Go Round	BQHO	6 Grid	183
Nuance		10 Grid	185
Paradise	BQHO	10 Grid	187
Pardon Me		8 Grid	189
Patchwork Ribbon		12 Grid	191
Pearl Appeal		8 Grid	193
Picnicking	BQHO	9 Grid	195
Pixie Dust		12 Grid	197
Plaid Star		8 Grid	199
Razzle Dazzle		8 Grid	201
Rival Sisters	BQHO	12 Grid	203
Seminole Star		12 Grid	205
Show It Off	BQHO	12 Grid	207

Directory of Patterns

Directory of Patterns

Advance Patterns	BQH Original	Grid Count	Page
My Sewing Passion	BQHO	24 Grid	271
Off Center		12 Grid	273
Palms		6 Grid	275
Panseys in the Spring		23 grid	277
Party Favors		15 Grid	279
Phoenix	BQHO	16 Grid	281
Piney Creek	BQHO	8 Grid	283
Prancing Peacock		16 Grid	285
Rose Garden	BQHO	16 Grid	287
Royality		16 Grid	289
Rustic Christmas	BQHO	16 Grid	291
Sally Sue		12 Grid	239
Sneaky Snails		12 Grid	295
Snowflake (Offset)		20 Grid	297
Sparkle, Sparkle	BQHO	16 Grid	299
Stunning Star		16 Grid	301
Tribal Star	BQHO	18 Grid	303
Under the Apple Tree		12 Grid	304
Very Merry Christmas		8 Grid	305
Vortex	BQHO	12 Grid	307
Waving Flag		12 Grid	309
Wildflower Seeds		24 Grid	311
Point Based		Degrees	
16 Point Star / Sunflower		22.5	313
Birthday Surprise		45	315
Demanding Attention		22.5	316
Dresden Daisy		15	317
Fan Me		15	319
Fancy Mosaic Star		20	321
Folded Pieced Bloom		45	323
Geometry 101	BQHO	15	325
Indian Star	BQHO	22.5	327
Mystic Star	BQHO	22.5	329
Wine & Dine	BQHO	22.5	331

Directory of Patterns

Circle Based Patterns		Grid	Page
Beautiful Baskets	BQHO	12 Grid	333
Blessed Cathedral	BQHO	10 Grid	335
Bobble	BQHO	6 Grid	337
Dahlia Bloom		30 Degrees	339
Family Affair	BQHO	10 Grid	341
Four Tulips		8 Grid	343
Glorious		4 Grid	345
Never Grow Up		4 Grid	347
Prairie Dust	BQHO	16 Grid	349
Sincere	BQHO	7 Grid	351
Vintage Romance	BQHO	12 Grid	353
Wedding Ring	BQHO	22.5 Degrees	355

Understanding The Pattern Illustrations

I tried my best to illustrate how to draw each pattern and if you have my previous book(s), you will notice I did not provide the grid red lines. I feel that this should be self-explanatory by now. If you don't, this book does not give step by step or materials as those do.

You will find that the broken dotted lines are the lines that are not drawn or are erased after drawing.

The red or green lines will indicate where you lay your straight edge to achieve the connecting lines to form the pattern.

I have tried to indicate with a red mark, your pivot points for the compass for circles.

I have given tips on a pattern to clarify what I deemed may be confusing however, all minds don't process info alike, so I hope what I tried helps.

Have fun and if you post a picture of your beautiful barn quilt on social media, don't forget to reference pattern name and where the pattern can be found for those that want to flatter by imitation!

Some of my work – and I can't wait to see yours!

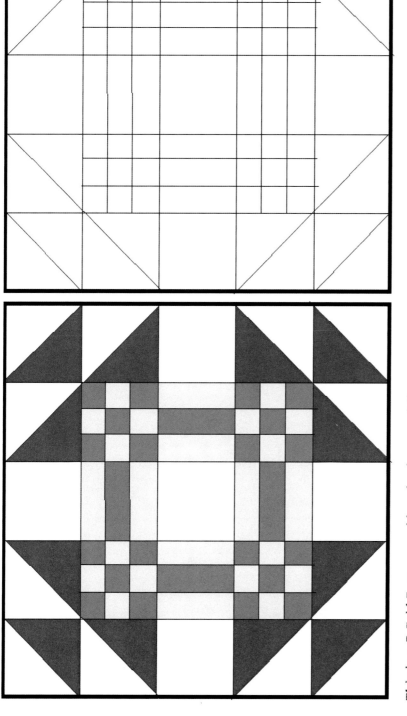

This is a 5 Grid Pattern and breaks down as follows:

It is recommended to place a border around this pattern for ease if you cannot divide evenly by 5.

2 x 2 - 4.75" grid pattern - slight border necessary

3 x 3 - 7" grid pattern - slight border necessary

4 x 4 - 9.5" grid pattern - slight border necessary

This pattern is an 8 Grid Pattern and breaks down as follows:

It is recommended to place a border around this pattern for ease if you cannot divide evenly by 8.

2 x 2 - 3" grid - no border necessary

3 x 3 - 4.5" grid - no border necessary

4 x 4 - 6" grid - no border necessary

Braided Ribbon   Beginner   13 Grid

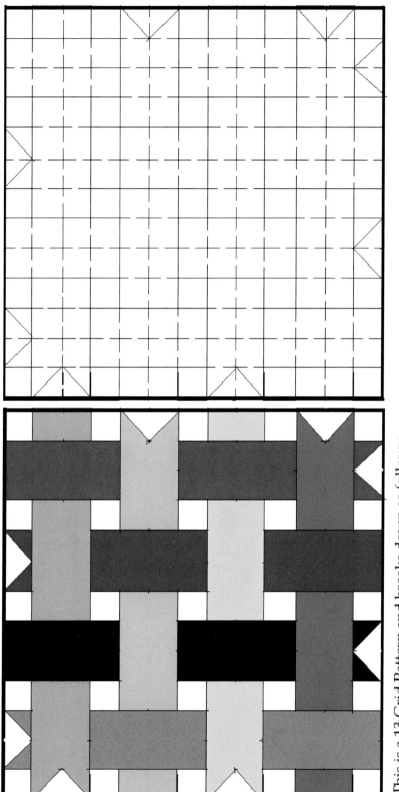

This is a 13 Grid Pattern and breaks down as follows:

It is recommended to place a border around this pattern for ease if you cannot divide evenly by 13.

2 x 2 – 1.75″ grid pattern – border necessary

3 x 3 – 2.75″ grid pattern – border necessary

4 x 4 – 3.5″ grid pattern – border necessary

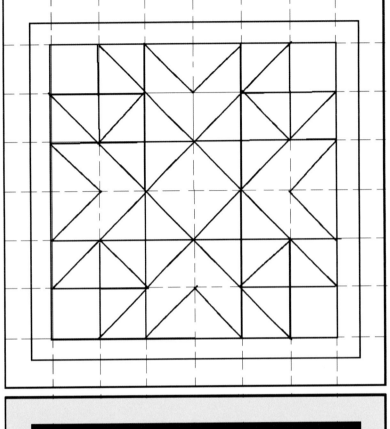

This pattern is an 8 Grid Pattern and breaks down as follows:

It is recommended to place a border around this pattern for ease if you cannot divide evenly by 8.

2 x 2 - 3" grid - no border necessary

3 x 3 - 4.5" grid - no border necessary

4 x 4 - 6" grid - no border necessary

Crown of Thorns   Beginner   5 Grid

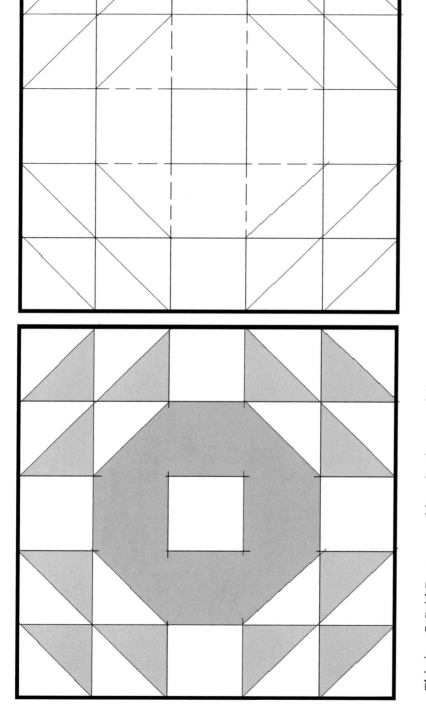

This is a 5 Grid Pattern and breaks down as follows:

It is recommended to place a border around this pattern for ease if you cannot divide evenly by 5.

2 x 2 - 4.75" grid pattern - slight border necessary

3 x 3 - 7" grid pattern - slight border necessary

4 x 4 - 9.5" grid pattern - slight border necessary

This is a 4 Grid Pattern and breaks down as follows:

It is recommended to place a border around this pattern for ease if you cannot divide evenly by 4.

2 x 2 - 6" grid pattern - no border necessary

3 x 3 - 9" grid pattern - no border necessary

4 x 4 - 12" grid pattern - no border necessary

Elaine's Block   Beginner   8 Grid

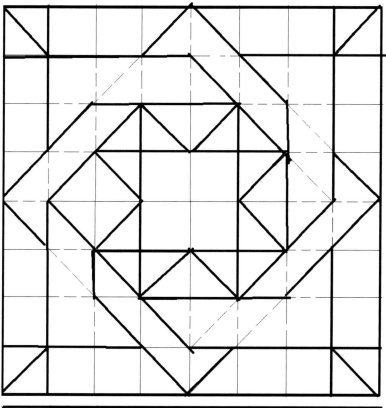

This pattern is an 8 Grid Pattern and breaks down as follows:

It is recommended to place a border around this pattern for ease if you cannot divide evenly by 8.

2 x 2 - 3" grid - no border necessary

3 x 3 - 4.5" grid - no border necessary

4 x 4 - 6" grid - no border necessary

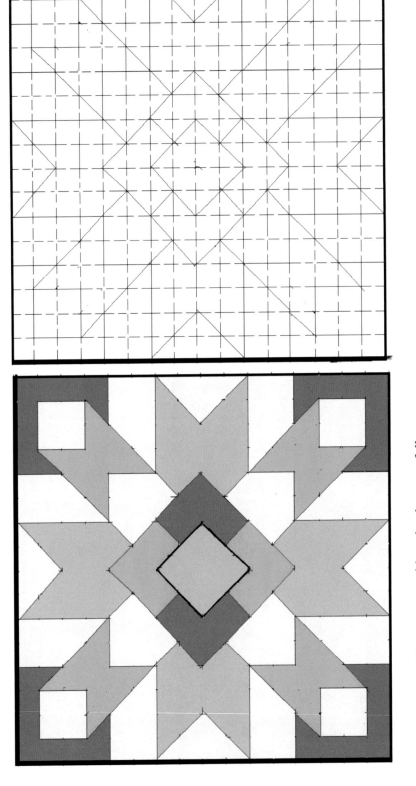

This is a 16 Grid Pattern and breaks down as follows:

It is recommeded to place a border around this pattern for ease if you cannot divide evenly by 16.

2 x 2 - 1.5" grid pattern - no border necessary

3 x 3 - 2.25 grid pattern - no border necessary

4 x 4 - 3" grid pattern - no border necessary

Tip: Divide the width of the four center blocks by 3 to get the stripes (shown in purple/navy).

This is a 5 Grid Pattern and breaks down as follows:

It is recommended to place a border around this pattern for ease if you cannot divide evenly by 5.

2 x 2 - 4.75" grid pattern - slight border necessary

3 x 3 - 7" grid pattern - slight border necessary

4 x 4 - 9.5" grid pattern - slight border necessary

Fancy Ribbon   Beginner   8 Grid

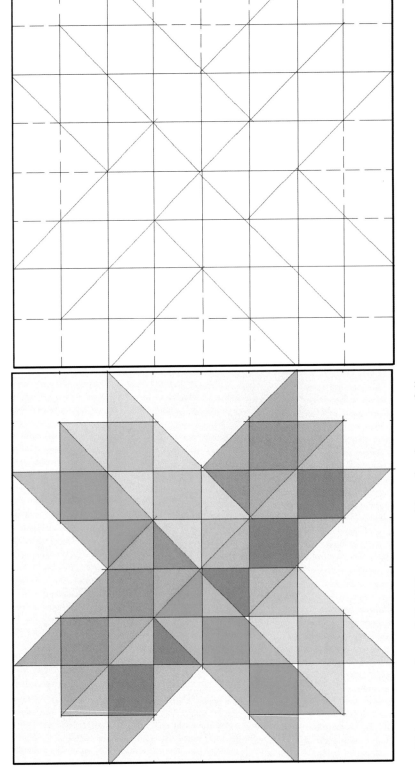

This pattern is an 8 Grid Pattern and breaks down as follows:

It is recommended to place a border around this pattern for ease if you cannot divide evenly by 8.

2 x 2 - 3" grid - no border necessary

3 x 3 - 4.5" grid - no border necessary

4 x 4 - 6" grid - no border necessary

Flywheel   Beginner   6 Grid

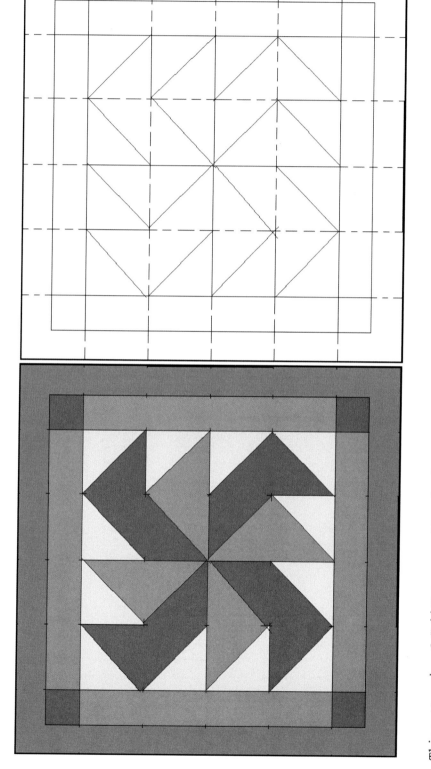

This pattern is a 6 Grid Pattern and breaks down as follows:

It is recommended to place a border around this pattern for ease if you cannot divide evenly by 6.

2 x 2 - 4" grid - no border necessary

3 x 3 - 6" grid - no border necessary

4 x 4 - 8" grid - no border necessary

Folk Art Star   Beginner   6 Grid

This pattern is a 6 Grid Pattern and breaks down as follows:

It is recommended to place a border around this pattern for ease if you cannot divide evenly by 6.

2 x 2 - 4" grid - no border necessary

3 x 3 - 6" grid - no border necessary

4 x 4 - 8" grid - no border necessary

This is a 4 Grid Pattern and breaks down as follows:

It is recommended to place a border around this pattern for ease if you cannot divide evenly by 4.

2 x 2 - 6" grid pattern - no border necessary

3 x 3 - 9" grid pattern - no border necessary

4 x 4 - 12" grid pattern - no border necessary

Tip: Print a star the size needed for the corner and trace out. Divide the three quads by the number of stripes you desire to get the width of those.

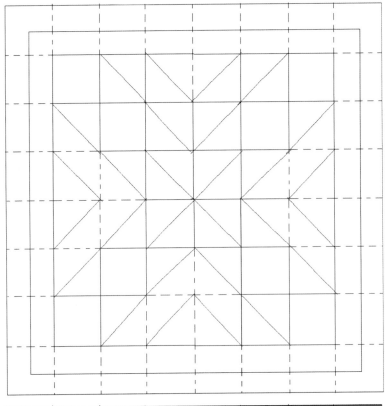

This pattern is an 8 Grid Pattern and breaks down as follows:

It is recommended to place a border around this pattern for ease if you cannot divide evenly by 8.

2 x 2 - 3" grid - no border necessary

3 x 3 - 4.5" grid - no border necessary

4 x 4 - 6" grid - no border necessary

This pattern is an 8 Grid Pattern and breaks down as follows:

It is recommended to place a border around this pattern for ease if you cannot divide evenly by 8.

2 x 2 - 3" grid - no border necessary

3 x 3 - 4.5" grid - no border necessary

4 x 4 - 6" grid - no border necessary

This pattern is a 6 Grid Pattern and breaks down as follows:

It is recommended to place a border around this pattern for ease if you cannot divide evenly by 6.

2 x 2 - 4" grid - no border necessary

3 x 3 - 6" grid - no border necessary

4 x 4 - 8" grid - no border necessary

Mezmerized   Beginner   8 Grid

This pattern is an 8 Grid Pattern and breaks down as follows:

It is recommended to place a border around this pattern for ease if you cannot divide evenly by 8.

2 x 2 - 3" grid - no border necessary

3 x 3 - 4.5" grid - no border necessary

4 x 4 - 6" grid - no border necessary

This pattern is an 8 Grid Pattern and breaks down as follows:

It is recommended to place a border around this pattern for ease if you cannot divide evenly by 8.

2 x 2 - 3" grid - no border necessary

3 x 3 - 4.5" grid - no border necessary

4 x 4 - 6" grid - no border necessary

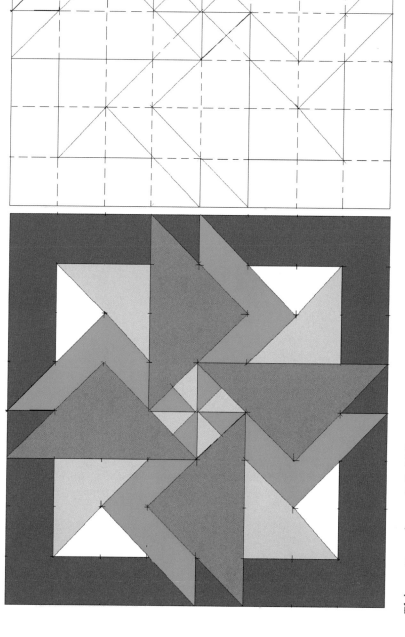

This pattern is an 8 Grid Pattern and breaks down as follows:

It is recommended to place a border around this pattern for ease if you cannot divide evenly by 8.

2 x 2 - 3" grid - no border necessary

3 x 3 - 4.5" grid - no border necessary

4 x 4 - 6" grid - no border necessary

Patchwork Sunflower   Beginner   8 Grid

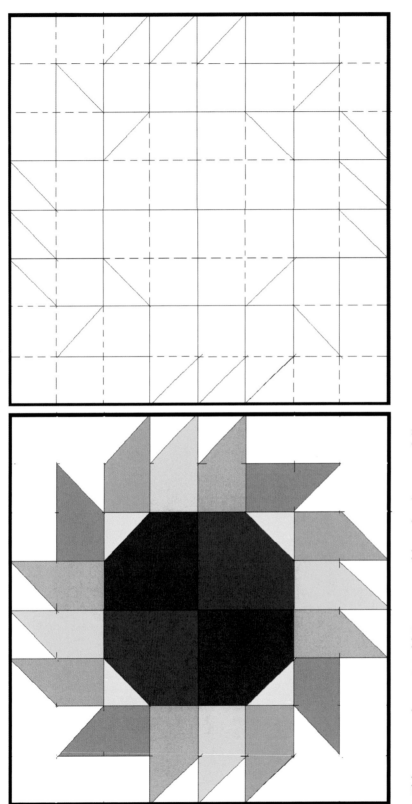

This pattern is an 8 Grid Pattern and breaks down as follows:

It is recommended to place a border around this pattern for ease if you cannot divide evenly by 8.

2 x 2 - 3" grid - no border necessary

3 x 3 - 4.5" grid - no border necessary

4 x 4 - 6" grid - no border necessary

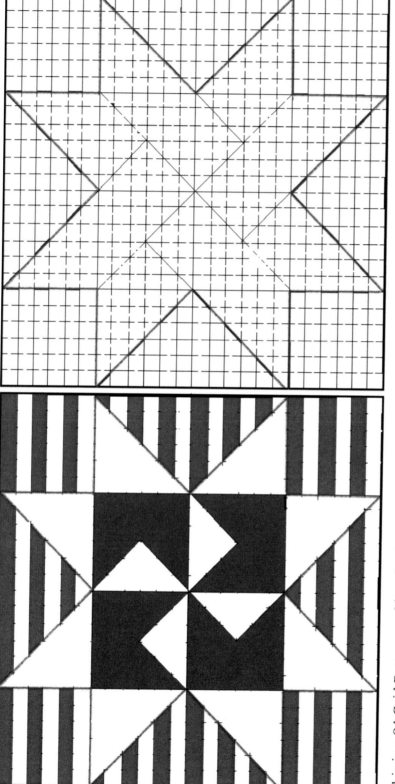

Patriot Sampler

Beginner

24 Grid

Tip: I would paint the entire board white first then draw the pattern off. Once you tape off the red lines, I recommend putting a coat of light grey paint before the red to help the color saturate.

This is a 24 Grid Pattern and breaks down as follows:

It is recommended to place a border around this pattern for ease if you cannot divide evenly by 24.

2 x 2 - 1" grid pattern - no border necessary

3 x 3 - 1.5" grid pattern - no border necessary

4 x 4 - 2" grid pattern - no border necessary

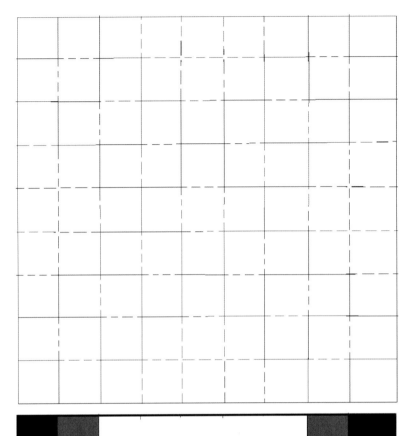

This pattern is a 9 Grid Pattern and breaks down as follows:

It is recommended to place a border around this pattern for ease if you cannot divide evenly by 9.

2 x 2 - 2.5" grid pattern - border necessary

3 x 3 - 4" grid pattern - no border necessary

4 x 4 - 5.25" grid pattern - border necessary

Rhododendron   Beginner   6 Grid

1/2 the grid makes border

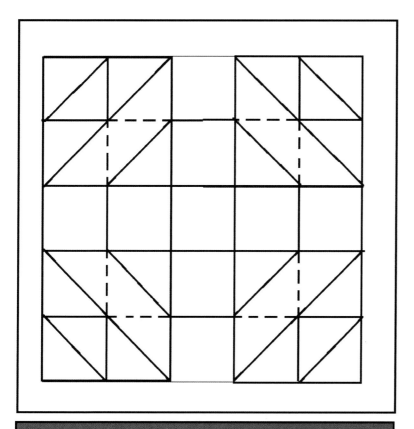

This pattern is a 6 Grid Pattern and breaks down as follows:

It is recommended to place a border around this pattern for ease if you cannot divide evenly by 6.

2 x 2 - 4" grid - no border necessary

3 x 3 - 6" grid - no border necessary

4 x 4 - 8" grid - no border necessary

Ribbons   Beginner   4 Grid

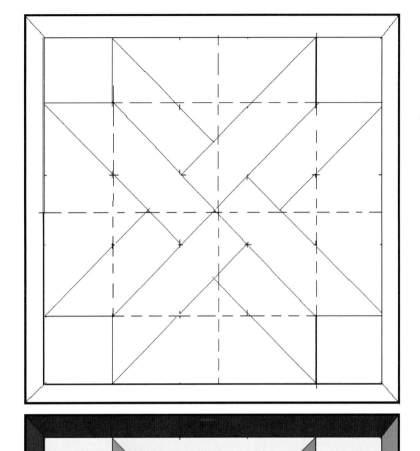

Tip: Reduce the grid size by the width you want your border. For instance, if you want a 1" border:

24-2 = 22"/4 = a grid of 5.5 for 2x2 size

This is a 4 Grid Pattern and breaks down as follows:

It is recommended to place a border around this pattern for ease if you cannot divide evenly by 4.

2 x 2 - 6" grid pattern - no border necessary

3 x 3 - 9" grid pattern - no border necessary

4 x 4 - 12" grid pattern - no border necessary

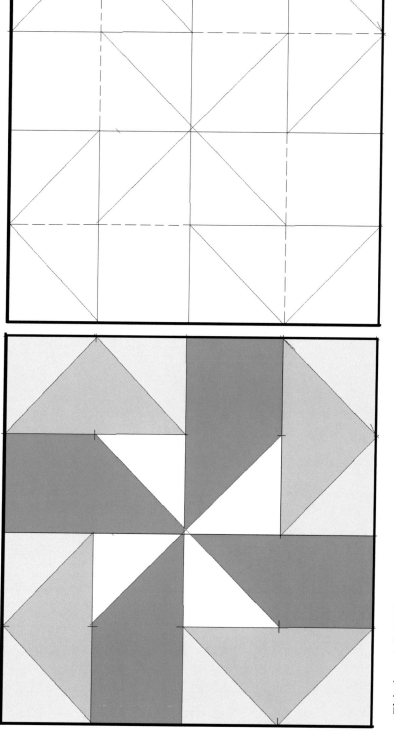

This is a 4 Grid Pattern and breaks down as follows:

It is recommended to place a border around this pattern for ease if you cannot divide evenly by 4.

2 x 2 - 6" grid pattern - no border necessary

3 x 3 - 9" grid pattern - no border necessary

4 x 4 - 12" grid pattern - no border necessary

Shining Star   Beginner   8 Grid

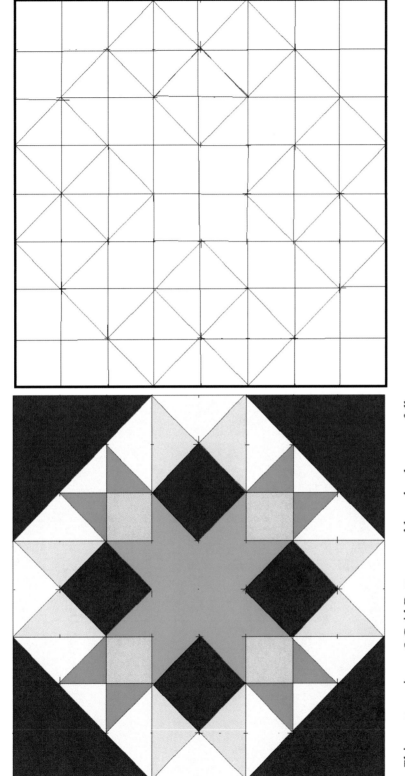

This pattern is an 8 Grid Pattern and breaks down as follows:

It is recommended to place a border around this pattern for ease if you cannot divide evenly by 8.

2 x 2 - 3" grid - no border necessary

3 x 3 - 4.5" grid - no border necessary

4 x 4 - 6" grid - no border necessary

Spools   Beginner   8 Grid

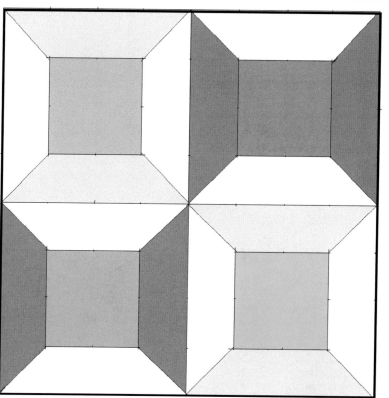

This pattern is an 8 Grid Pattern and breaks down as follows:

It is recommended to place a border around this pattern for ease if you cannot divide evenly by 8.

2 x 2 - 3" grid - no border necessary

3 x 3 - 4.5" grid - no border necessary

4 x 4 - 6" grid - no border necessary

This pattern is an 8 Grid Pattern and breaks down as follows:

It is recommended to place a border around this pattern for ease if you cannot divide evenly by 8.

2 x 2 - 3" grid - no border necessary

3 x 3 - 4.5" grid - no border necessary

4 x 4 - 6" grid - no border necessary

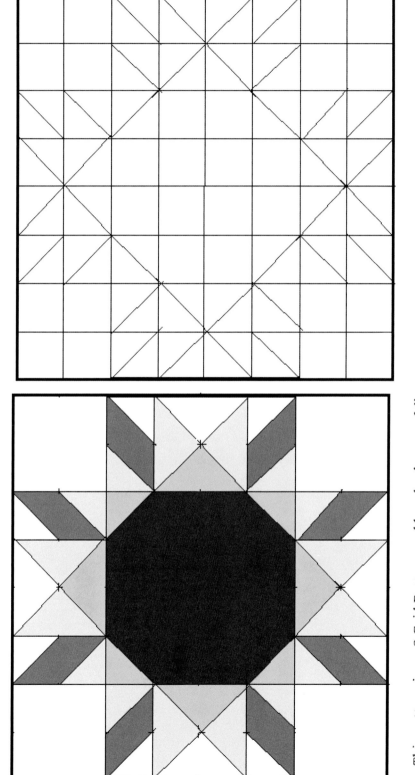

This pattern is an 8 Grid Pattern and breaks down as follows:

It is recommended to place a border around this pattern for ease if you cannot divide evenly by 8.

2 x 2 - 3" grid - no border necessary

3 x 3 - 4.5" grid - no border necessary

4 x 4 - 6" grid - no border necessary

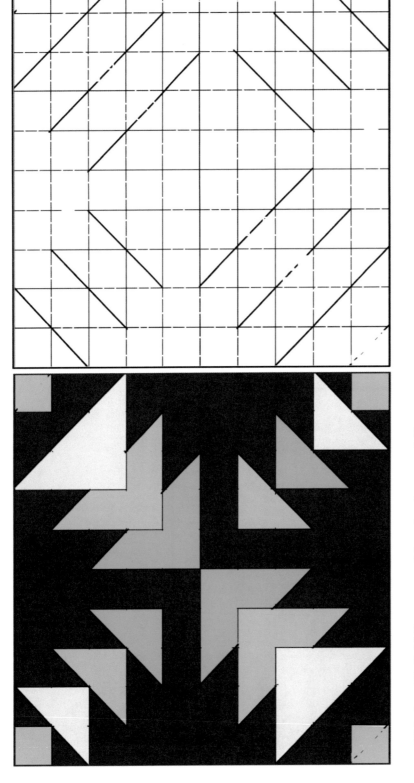

This is a 10 Grid Pattern and breaks down as follows:

It is recommended to place a border around this pattern for ease if you cannot divide evenly by 10.

2 x 2 - 2.25" grid pattern - .75" border necessary

3 x 3 - 3.5" grid pattern - .50" border necessary

4 x 4 - 4.75" grid pattern - slight border necessary

66

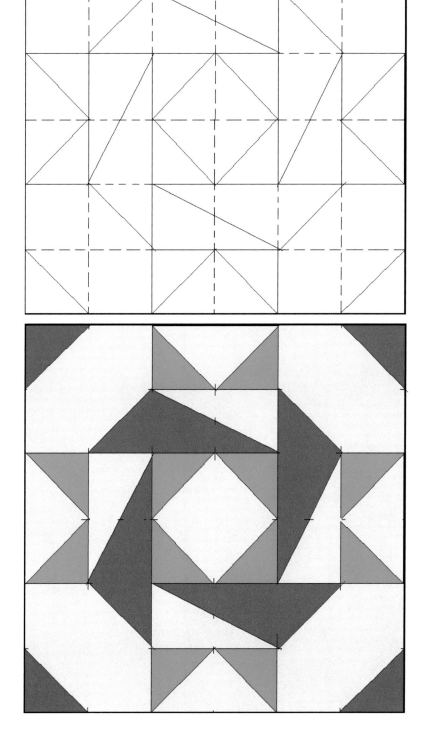

This pattern is a 6 Grid Pattern and breaks down as follows:

It is recommended to place a border around this pattern for ease if you cannot divide evenly by 6.

2 x 2 - 4" grid - no border necessary

3 x 3 - 6" grid - no border necessary

4 x 4 - 8" grid - no border necessary

67

Unity Star   Beginner   8 Grid

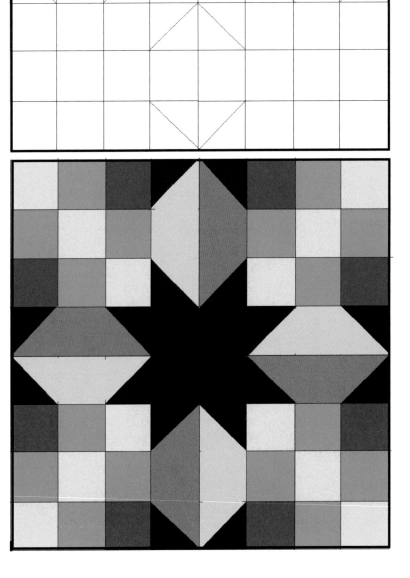

This pattern is an 8 Grid Pattern and breaks down as follows:

It is recommended to place a border around this pattern for ease if you cannot divide evenly by 8.

2 x 2 - 3" grid - no border necessary

3 x 3 - 4.5" grid - no border necessary

4 x 4 - 6" grid - no border necessary

Windmill   Beginner   5 Grid

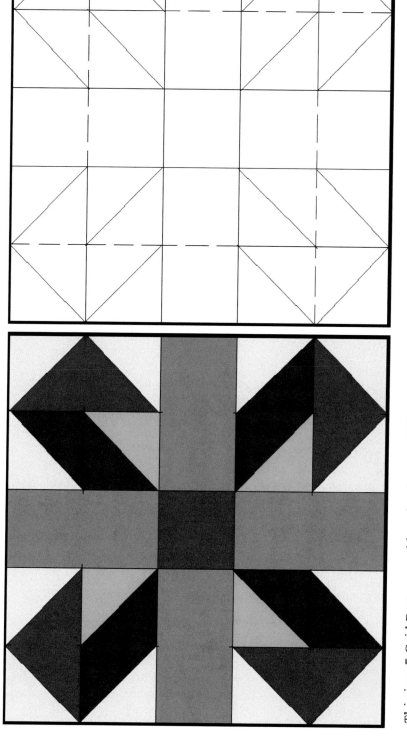

This is a 5 Grid Pattern and breaks down as follows:

It is recommended to place a border around this pattern for ease if you cannot divide evenly by 5.

2 x 2 - 4.75" grid pattern - slight border necessary

3 x 3 - 7" grid pattern - slight border necessary

4 x 4 - 9.5" grid pattern - slight border necessary

Wisconsin   Beginner   5 Grid

This is a 5 Grid Pattern and breaks down as follows:

It is recommended to place a border around this pattern for ease if you cannot divide evenly by 5.

2 x 2 - 4.75" grid pattern - slight border necessary

3 x 3 - 7" grid pattern - slight border necessary

4 x 4 - 9.5" grid pattern - slight border necessary

e

"No one can paint just one."

— Wende Hughson

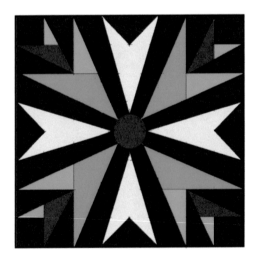

This pattern is an 8 Grid Pattern and breaks down as follows:

It is recommended to place a border around this pattern for ease if you cannot divide evenly by 8.

2 x 2 - 3" grid - no border necessary

3 x 3 - 4.5" grid - no border necessary

4 x 4 - 6" grid - no border necessary

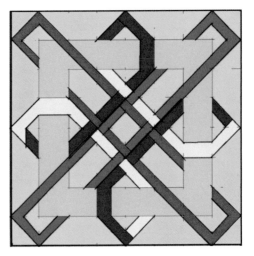

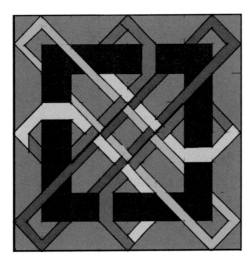

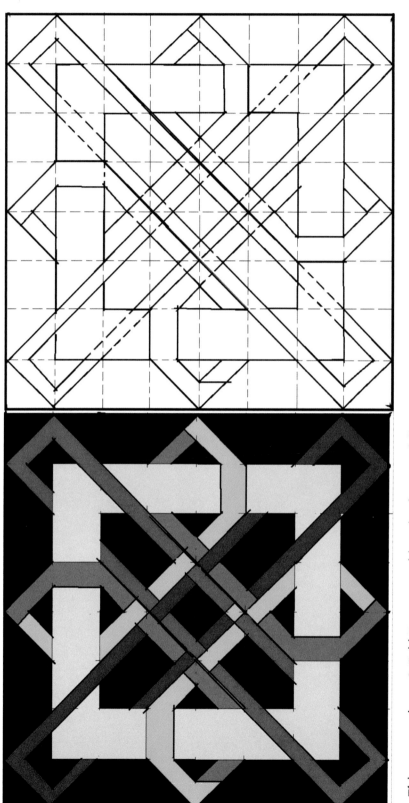

This pattern is an 8 Grid Pattern and breaks down as follows:

It is recommended to place a border around this pattern for ease if you cannot divide evenly by 8.

2 x 2 - 3" grid - no border necessary

3 x 3 - 4.5" grid - no border necessary

4 x 4 - 6" grid - no border necessary

This is a 10 Grid Pattern and breaks down as follows:

It is recommended to place a border around this pattern for ease if you cannot divide evenly by 10.

2 x 2 - 2.25" grid pattern - .75" border necessary

3 x 3 - 3.5" grid pattern - .50" border necessary

4 x 4 - 4.75" grid pattern - slight border necessary

This is a 11 Grid Pattern and breaks down as follows:

It is recommended to place a boarder around this pattern for ease if you cannot divide evenly by 11.

2 x 2 – 2" grid pattern – border necessary

3 x 3 – 3.25" grid pattern – border necessary

4 x 4 – 4.25" grid pattern – border necessary

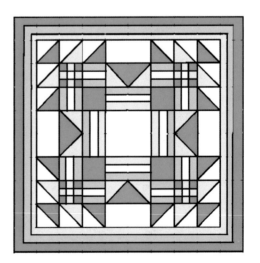

This is a 12 Grid Pattern and breaks down as follows:

It is recommended to place a border around this pattern for ease if you cannot divide evenly by 12.

2 x 2 - 2" grid pattern - no border necessary

3 x 3 - 3" grid pattern - no border necessary

4 x 4 - 4" grid pattern - no border necessary

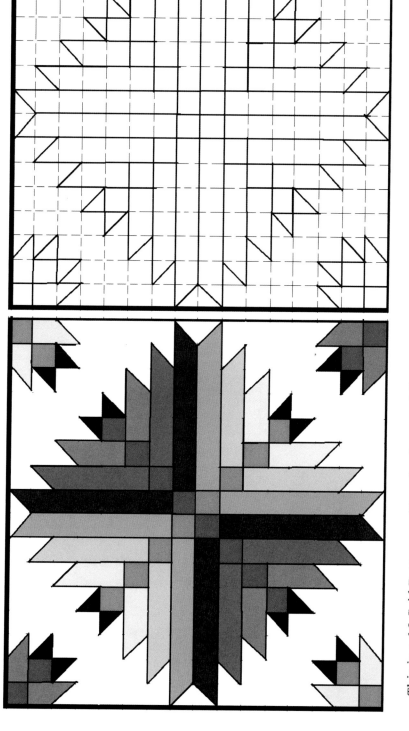

This is a 16 Grid Pattern and breaks down as follows:

It is recommeded to place a border around this pattern for ease if you cannot divide evenly by 16.

2 x 2 - 1.5" grid pattern - no border necessary

3 x 3 - 2.25 grid pattern - no border necessary

4 x 4 - 3" grid pattern - no border necessary

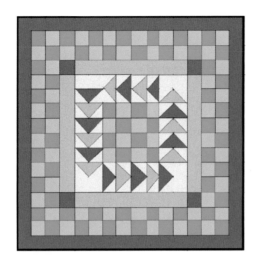

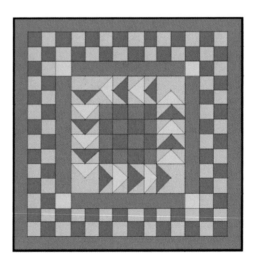

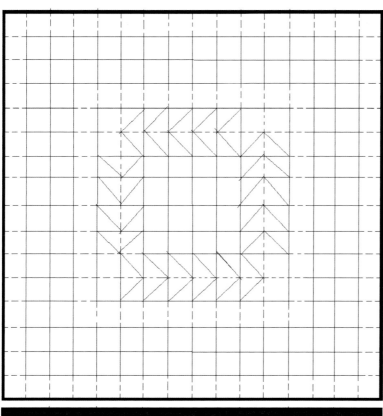

This is a 16 Grid Pattern and breaks down as follows:

It is recommeded to place a border around this pattern for ease if you cannot divide evenly by 16.

2 x 2 - 1.5" grid pattern - no border necessary

3 x 3 - 2.25 grid pattern - no border necessary

4 x 4 - 3" grid pattern - no border necessary

Barn Quilt Queen's Crown   BQHO   Intermediate   12 Grid

This is a 12 Grid Pattern and breaks down as follows:

It is recommended to place a border around this pattern for ease if you cannot divide evenly by 12.

2 x 2 - 2" grid pattern - no border necessary

3 x 3 - 3" grid pattern - no border necessary

4 x 4 - 4" grid pattern - no border necessary

This pattern is an 8 Grid Pattern and breaks down as follows:

It is recommended to place a border around this pattern for ease if you cannot divide evenly by 8.

2 x 2 - 3" grid - no border necessary

3 x 3 - 4.5" grid - no border necessary

4 x 4 - 6" grid - no border necessary

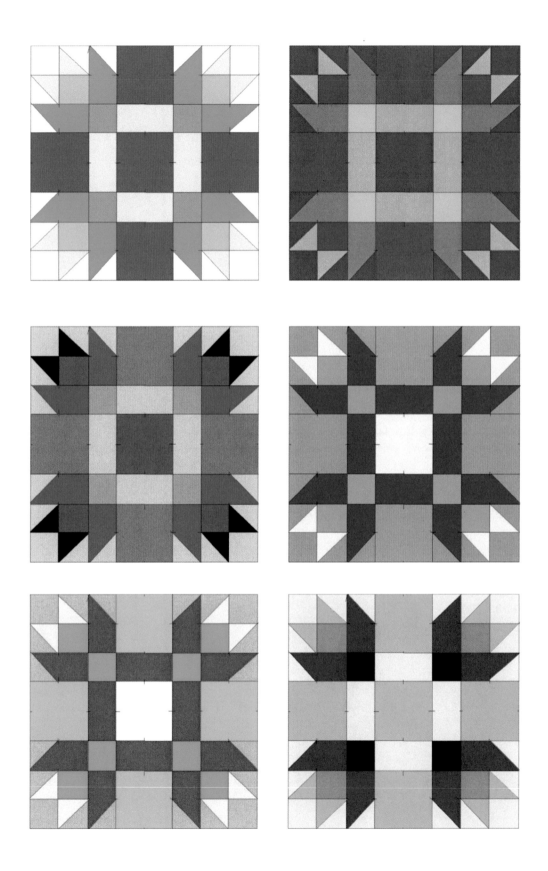

Bear Cub   Intermediate   8 Grid

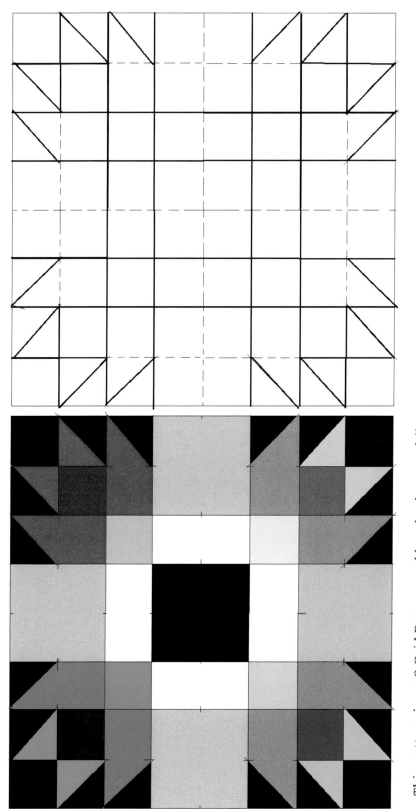

This pattern is an 8 Grid Pattern and breaks down as follows:

It is recommended to place a border around this pattern for ease if you cannot divide evenly by 8.

2 x 2 - 3" grid - no border necessary

3 x 3 - 4.5" grid - no border necessary

4 x 4 - 6" grid - no border necessary

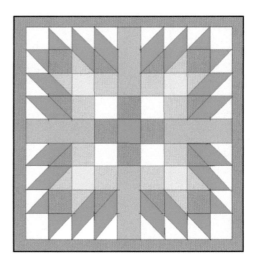

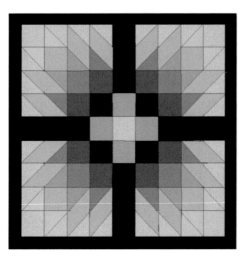

94

Bear Trap   Intermediate   10 Grid

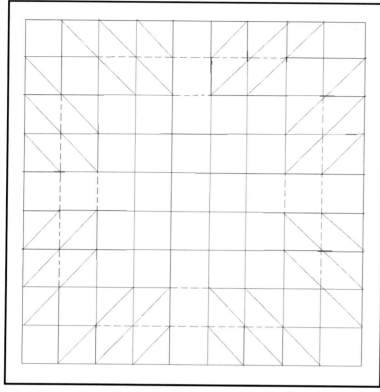

Tip: The 10th grid is divided in half and placed on the outside edge to form the border.

This is a 10 Grid Pattern and breaks down as follows:

It is recommended to place a border around this pattern for ease if you cannot divide evenly by 10.

2 x 2 - 2.25" grid pattern - .75" border necessary

3 x 3 - 3.5" grid pattern - .50" border necessary

4 x 4 - 4.75" grid pattern - slight border necessary

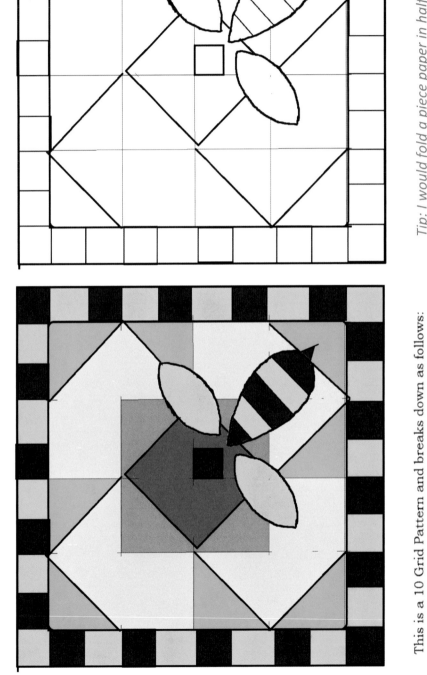

Tip: I would fold a piece paper in half and cut out the shapes, opening and then placing in the pattern. Once satisfied, trace around, tape and trim out, paint.

This is a 10 Grid Pattern and breaks down as follows:

It is recommended to place a border around this pattern for ease if you cannot divide evenly by 10.

2 x 2 - 2.25" grid pattern - .75" border necessary

3 x 3 - 3.5" grid pattern - .50" border necessary

4 x 4 - 4.75" grid pattern - slight border necessary

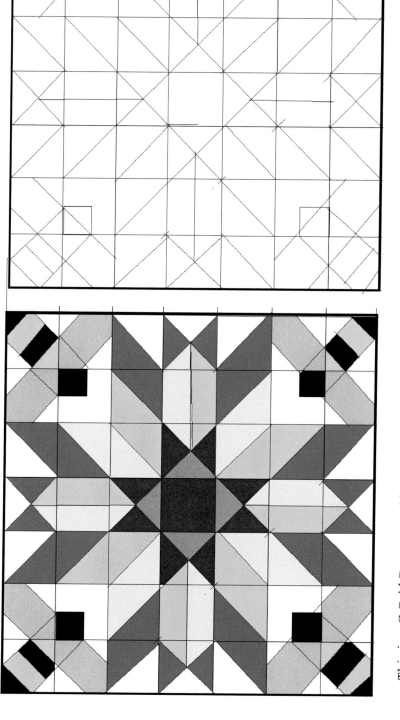

This is a 7 Grid Pattern and breaks down as follows:

It is recommended to place a border around this pattern for ease if you cannot divide evenly by 7.

2 x 2 - 3.25" grid pattern - border necessary

3 x 3 - 5" grid pattern - border necessary

4 x 4 - 6.75 grid pattern - border necessary

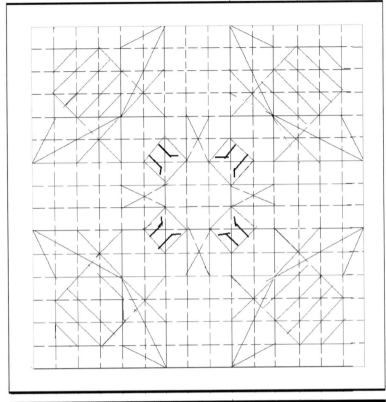

This is a 17 Grid Pattern and breaks down as follows:

It is recommended to place a boarder around this pattern for ease if you cannot divide evenly by 17.

2 x 2 – 1.25″ grid pattern – border necessary

3 x 3 – 2″ grid pattern – border necessary

4 x 4 – 2.75″ grid pattern – border necessary

e

"You don't have to know how to paint you you just need to want to paint" -

Deborah May

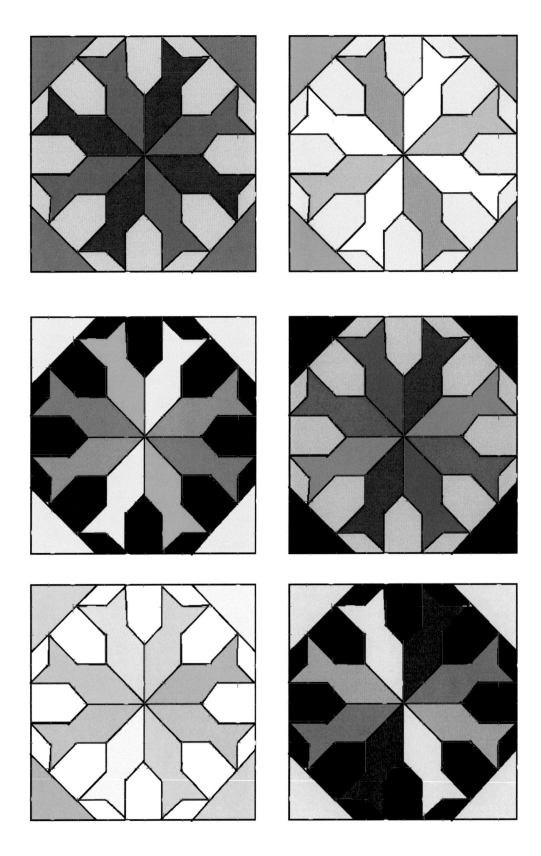

9 Patch Ladder   Intermediate   8 Grid

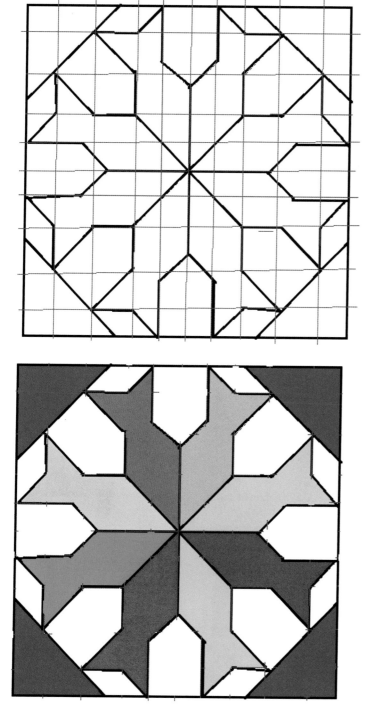

This is an 8 grid pattern but you start with the first grid cut in half on each side of the board and then measure out.   The other half of the grid is at the edges.

For instance, if a 2 x 2 , , start from the center of edge and measure out 1.5", then 3" there after. Last measurement will be 1.5". Repeat on other side then on all 4 sides of the board.

To get the size of your grid, take the size of your board and divide it by 8.

This pattern is an 8 Grid Pattern and breaks down as follows:

It is recommended to place a border around this pattern for ease if you cannot divide evenly by 8.

2 x 2 - 3" grid - no border necessary

3 x 3 - 4.5" grid - no border necessary

4 x 4 - 6" grid - no border necessary

e

"Creativity is a drug I cannot live without." – Cecil B. DeMille

Cardinal Pair   Intermediate   7 Grid

This is a 7 Grid Pattern and breaks down as follows:

It is recommended to place a border around this pattern for ease if you cannot divide evenly by 7.

2 x 2 - 3.25" grid pattern - border necessary

3 x 3 - 5" grid pattern - border necessary

4 x 4 - 6.75 grid pattern - border necessary

Tip: The 7th grid is divided in half to make the border on this pattern.

105

This pattern is a 14 Grid Pattern and breaks down as follows:

It is recommended to place a border around this pattern for ease if you cannot divide evenly by 14.

2 x 2 - 1.625 (1 5/8") grid pattern - border necessary

3 x 3 - 2.5" grid pattern - border necessary

4 x 4 - 3.25" grid pattern - border necessary

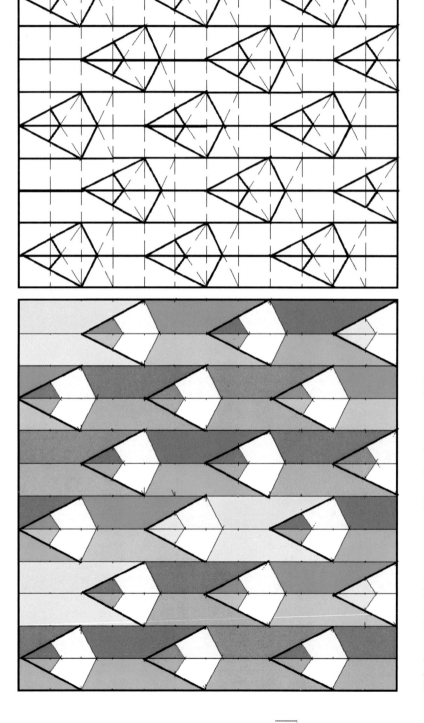

This is a 12 Grid Pattern and breaks down as follows:

It is recommended to place a border around this pattern for ease if you cannot divide evenly by 12.

2 x 2 - 2" grid pattern - no border necessary

3 x 3 - 3" grid pattern - no border necessary

4 x 4 - 4" grid pattern - no border necessary

e

"Those who do not want to imitate anything, produce nothing."

— Salvador Dali

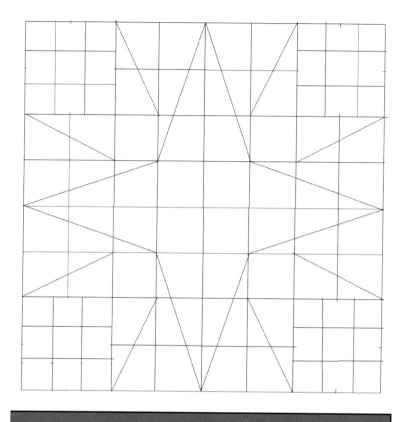

Tip: The four grids are broken done into 3 grids on the corners and two on the center grids.

This is a 4 Grid Pattern and breaks down as follows:

It is recommended to place a border around this pattern for ease if you cannot divide evenly by 4.

2 x 2 - 6" grid pattern - no border necessary

3 x 3 - 9" grid pattern - no border necessary

4 x 4 - 12" grid pattern - no border necessary

Cutie Patootie   Beginner   8 Grid

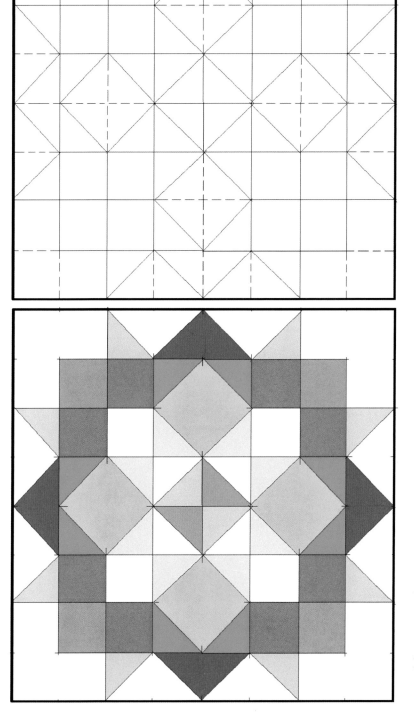

This pattern is an 8 Grid Pattern and breaks down as follows:

It is recommended to place a border around this pattern for ease if you cannot divide evenly by 8.

2 x 2 - 3" grid - no border necessary

3 x 3 - 4.5" grid - no border necessary

4 x 4 - 6" grid - no border necessary

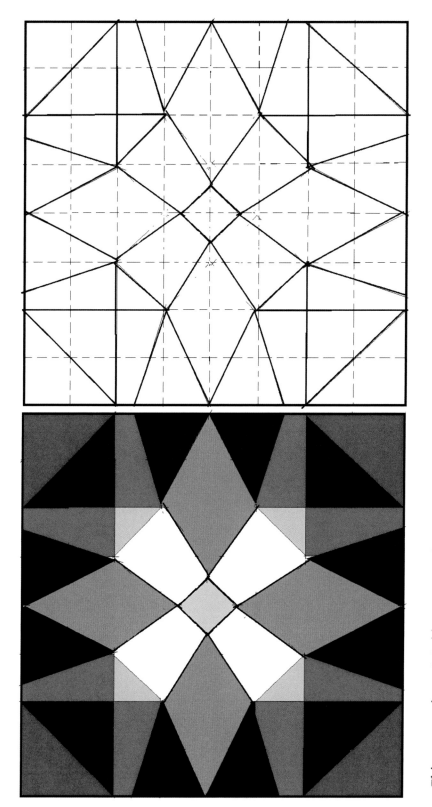

This pattern is an 8 Grid Pattern and breaks down as follows:

It is recommended to place a border around this pattern for ease if you cannot divide evenly by 8.

2 x 2 - 3" grid - no border necessary

3 x 3 - 4.5" grid - no border necessary

4 x 4 - 6" grid - no border necessary

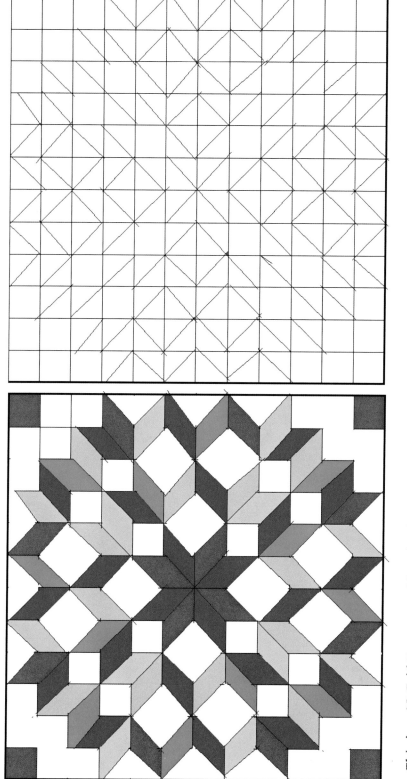

This is a 12 Grid Pattern and breaks down as follows:

It is recommended to place a border around this pattern for ease if you cannot divide evenly by 12.

2 x 2 - 2" grid pattern - no border necessary

3 x 3 - 3" grid pattern - no border necessary

4 x 4 - 4" grid pattern - no border necessary

This pattern is an 8 Grid Pattern and breaks down as follows:

It is recommended to place a border around this pattern for ease if you cannot divide evenly by 8.

2 x 2 - 3" grid - no border necessary

3 x 3 - 4.5" grid - no border necessary

4 x 4 - 6" grid - no border necessary

This pattern is an 8 Grid Pattern and breaks down as follows:

It is recommended to place a border around this pattern for ease if you cannot divide evenly by 8.

2 x 2 - 3" grid - no border necessary

3 x 3 - 4.5" grid - no border necessary

4 x 4 - 6" grid - no border necessary

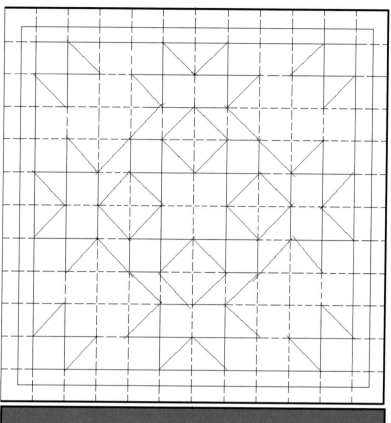

This is a 12 Grid Pattern and breaks down as follows:

It is recommended to place a border around this pattern for ease if you cannot divide evenly by 12.

2 x 2 - 2" grid pattern - no border necessary

3 x 3 - 3" grid pattern - no border necessary

4 x 4 - 4" grid pattern - no border necessary

This is a 12 Grid Pattern and breaks down as follows:

It is recommended to place a border around this pattern for ease if you cannot divide evenly by 12.

2 x 2 - 2" grid pattern - no border necessary

3 x 3 - 3" grid pattern - no border necessary

4 x 4 - 4" grid pattern - no border necessary

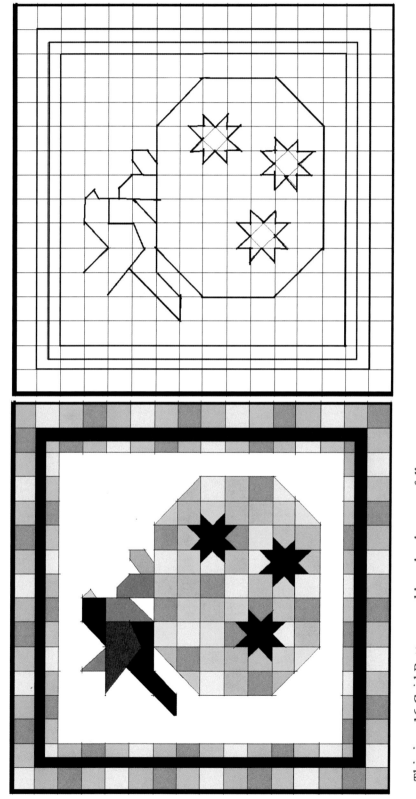

This is a 16 Grid Pattern and breaks down as follows:

It is recommeded to place a border around this pattern for ease if you cannot divide evenly by 16.

2 x 2 - 1.5" grid pattern - no border necessary

3 x 3 - 2.25 grid pattern - no border necessary

4 x 4 - 3" grid pattern - no border necessary

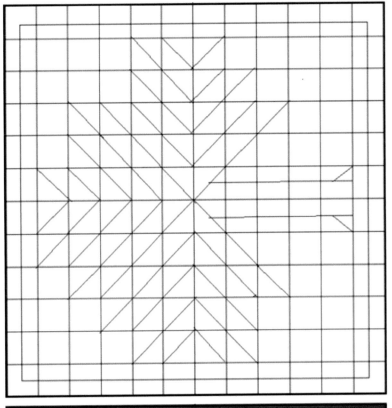

This is a 12 Grid Pattern and breaks down as follows:

It is recommended to place a border around this pattern for ease if you cannot divide evenly by 12.

2 x 2 - 2" grid pattern - no border necessary

3 x 3 - 3" grid pattern - no border necessary

4 x 4 - 4" grid pattern - no border necessary

Father's Choice   Intermediate   5 Grid

This is a 5 Grid Pattern and breaks down as follows:

It is recommended to place a border around this pattern for ease if you cannot divide evenly by 5.

2 x 2 - 4.75" grid pattern - slight border necessary

3 x 3 - 7" grid pattern - slight border necessary

4 x 4 - 9.5" grid pattern - slight border necessary

 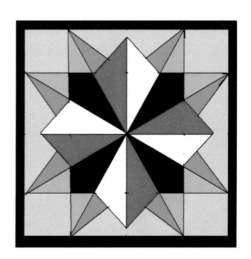

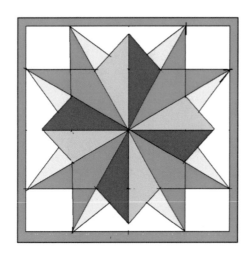 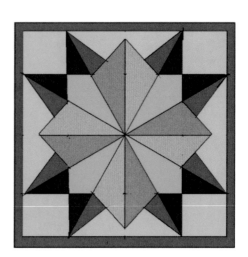

Farmer's Wife   Intermediate   4 Grid

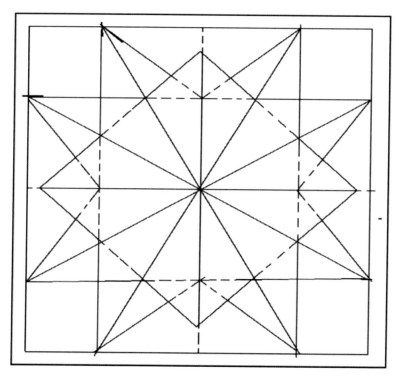

This is a 4 Grid Pattern and breaks down as follows:

It is recommended to place a border around this pattern for ease if you cannot divide evenly by 4.

2 x 2 - 6" grid pattern - no border necessary

3 x 3 - 9" grid pattern - no border necessary

4 x 4 - 12" grid pattern - no border necessary

This pattern is an 8 Grid Pattern and breaks down as follows:

It is recommended to place a border around this pattern for ease if you cannot divide evenly by 8.

2 x 2 - 3" grid - no border necessary

3 x 3 - 4.5" grid - no border necessary

4 x 4 - 6" grid - no border necessary

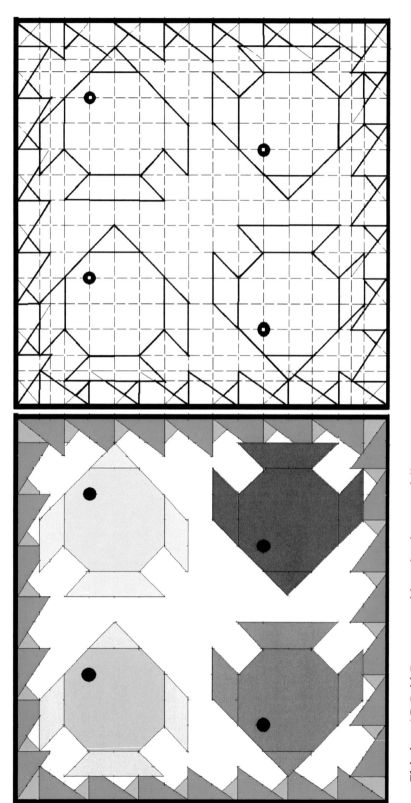

This is a 15 Grid Pattern and breaks down as follows:

It is recommended to place a border around this pattern for ease if you cannot divide evenly by 15

2 x 2 - 1.5" grid pattern - .75" border necessary

3 x 3 - 2.25" grid pattern - 1" border necessary

4 x 4 - 3" grid pattern - 1.5" border necessary

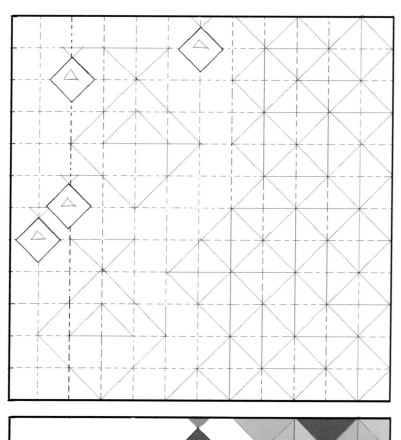

This is a 12 Grid Pattern and breaks down as follows:

It is recommended to place a border around this pattern for ease if you cannot divide evenly by 12.

2 x 2 - 2" grid pattern - no border necessary

3 x 3 - 3" grid pattern - no border necessary

4 x 4 - 4" grid pattern - no border necessary

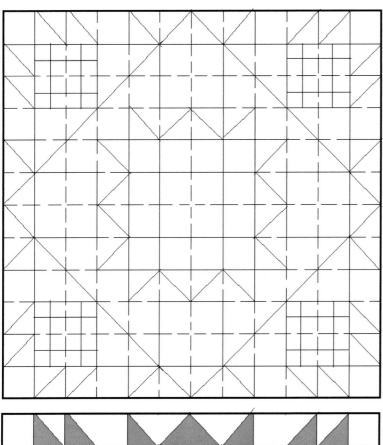

This is a 12 Grid Pattern and breaks down as follows:

It is recommended to place a border around this pattern for ease if you cannot divide evenly by 12.

2 x 2 - 2" grid pattern - no border necessary

3 x 3 - 3" grid pattern - no border necessary

4 x 4 - 4" grid pattern - no border necessary

This pattern is a 6 Grid Pattern and breaks down as follows:

It is recommended to place a border around this pattern for ease if you cannot divide evenly by 6.

2 x 2 - 4" grid - no border necessary

3 x 3 - 6" grid - no border necessary

4 x 4 - 8" grid - no border necessary

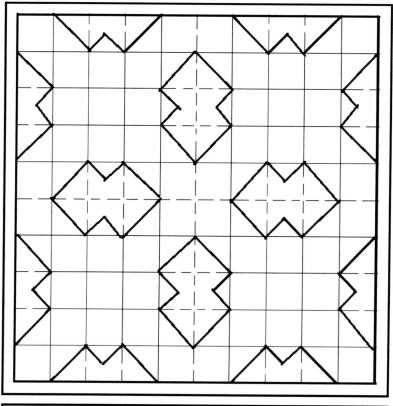

This is a 10 Grid Pattern and breaks down as follows:

It is recommended to place a border around this pattern for ease if you cannot divide evenly by 10.

2 x 2 - 2.25" grid pattern - .75" border necessary

3 x 3 - 3.5" grid pattern - .50" border necessary

4 x 4 - 4.75" grid pattern - slight border necessary

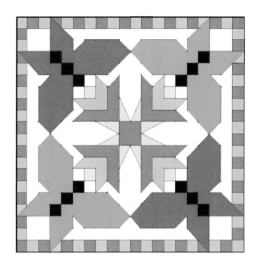 

Painted by Deborah May of Barn Quilt Express, located in Coweta, Ok. Officially the first barn quilt of this design. Thank you for choosing this design. Beautiful work.

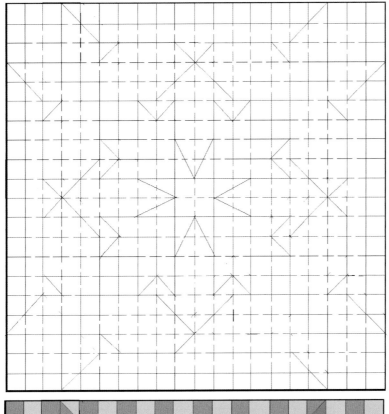

This pattern is a 20 Grid Pattern and breaks down as follows:

It is recommended to place a border around this pattern for ease if you cannot divide evenly by 20.

2 x 2 - 1.13 (1 1/8") grid pattern - See Tip

3 x 3 - 1.75" grid pattern - See Tip

4 x 4 - 2.25" grid pattern - no border necessary

e

"Creativity is contagious,

pass it on."

— Albert Einstein

4 Leaf Clover   Intermediate   15 Grid

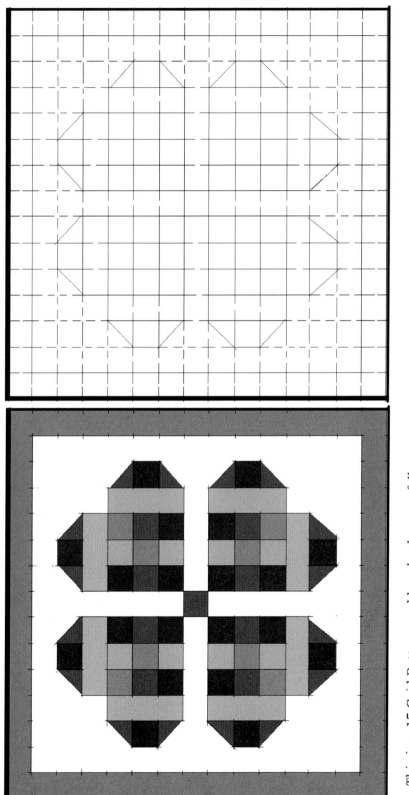

This is a 15 Grid Pattern and breaks down as follows:

It is recommended to place a border around this pattern for ease if you cannot divide evenly by 15

2 x 2 - 1.5" grid pattern - .75" border necessary

3 x 3 - 2.25" grid pattern - 1" border necessary

4 x 4 - 3" grid pattern - 1.5" border necessary

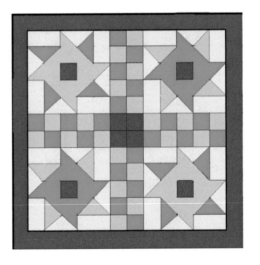

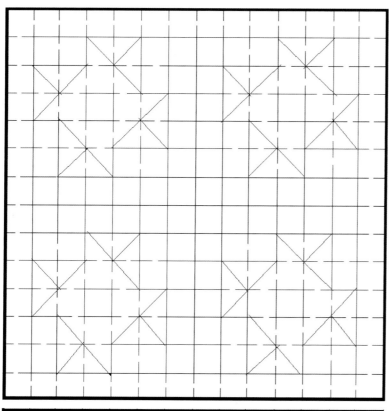

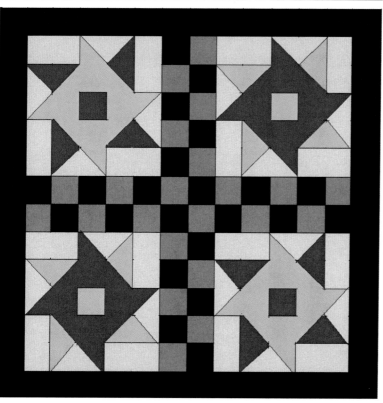

This pattern is a 14 Grid Pattern and breaks down as follows:

It is recommended to place a border around this pattern for ease if you cannot divide evenly by 14.

2 x 2 - 1.625 (1 5/8") grid pattern - border necessary

3 x 3 - 2.5" grid pattern - border necessary

4 x 4 - 3.25" grid pattern - border necessary

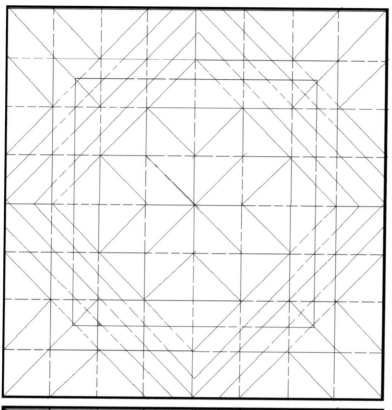

This pattern is an 8 Grid Pattern and breaks down as follows:

It is recommended to place a border around this pattern for ease if you cannot divide evenly by 8.

2 x 2 - 3" grid - no border necessary

3 x 3 - 4.5" grid - no border necessary

4 x 4 - 6" grid - no border necessary

e

"Art enables us to find ourselves and lose ourselves at the same time."

— Thomas Merton

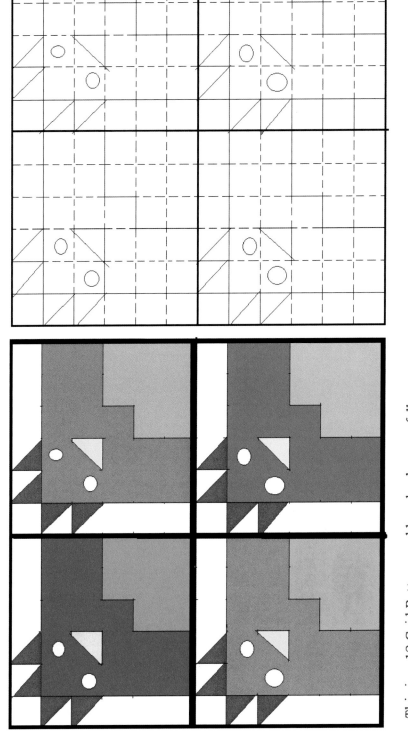

This is a 12 Grid Pattern and breaks down as follows:

It is recommended to place a border around this pattern for ease if you cannot divide evenly by 12.

2 x 2 - 2" grid pattern - no border necessary

3 x 3 - 3" grid pattern - no border necessary

4 x 4 - 4" grid pattern - no border necessary

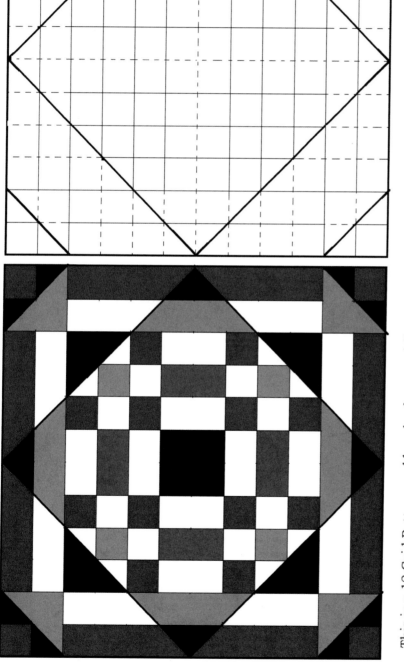

This is a 12 Grid Pattern and breaks down as follows:

It is recommended to place a border around this pattern for ease if you cannot divide evenly by 12.

2 x 2 - 2" grid pattern - no border necessary

3 x 3 - 3" grid pattern - no border necessary

4 x 4 - 4" grid pattern - no border necessary

Guardian Angel   BQHO   Intermediate   20 Grid

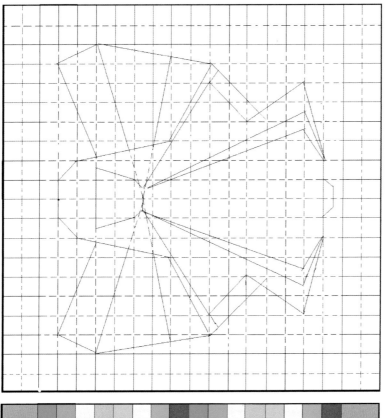

Tip: Always round your measurement down to the nearest 1/8" if you cannot divide evenly.

This pattern is a 20 Grid Pattern and breaks down as follows:

It is recommended to place a border around this pattern for ease if you cannot divide evenly by 20.

2 x 2 - 1.13 (1 1/8") grid pattern - See Tip

3 x 3 - 1.75" grid pattern - See Tip

4 x 4 - 2.25" grid pattern - no border necessary

e

You can't use up creativity. The more you use, the more you have. – Unknown

Happy Little Camper   Intermediate   8 Grid

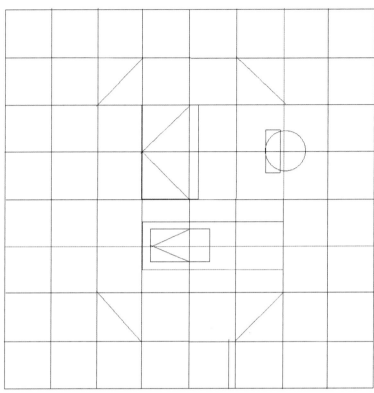

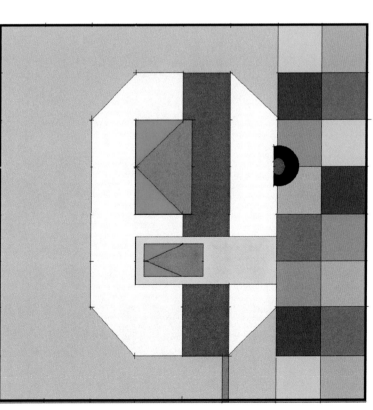

This pattern is an 8 Grid Pattern and breaks down as follows:

It is recommended to place a border around this pattern for ease if you cannot divide evenly by 8.

2 x 2 - 3" grid - no border necessary

3 x 3 - 4.5" grid - no border necessary

4 x 4 - 6" grid - no border necessary

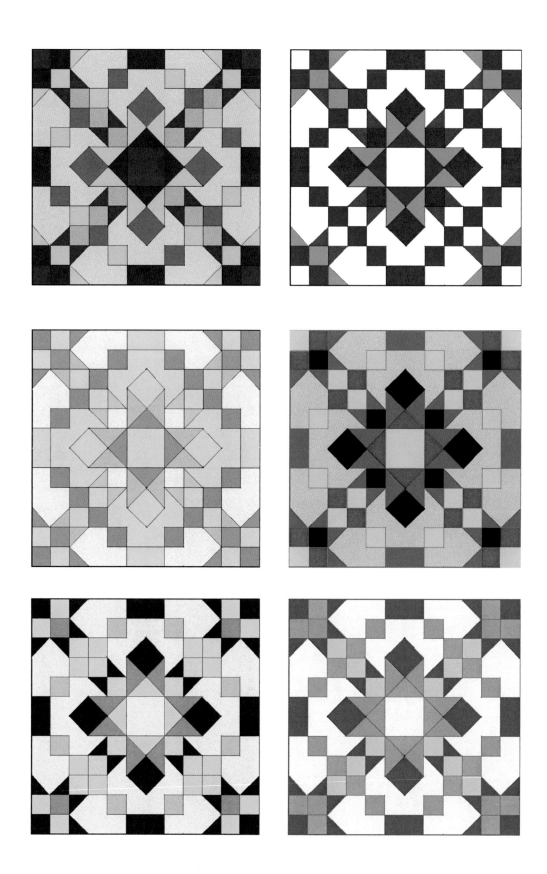

Heritage   BQHO   Intermediate   12 Grid

This is a 12 Grid Pattern and breaks down as follows:

It is recommended to place a border around this pattern for ease if you cannot divide evenly by 12.

2 x 2 - 2" grid pattern - no border necessary

3 x 3 - 3" grid pattern - no border necessary

4 x 4 - 4" grid pattern - no border necessary

157

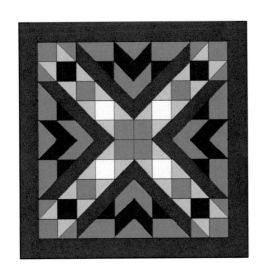

Homestead Star BQHO　　　　Intermediate　　　　12 Grid

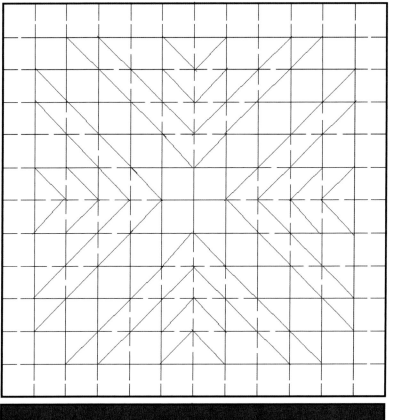

This is a 12 Grid Pattern and breaks down as follows:

It is recommended to place a border around this pattern for ease if you cannot divide evenly by 12.

2 x 2 - 2" grid pattern - no border necessary

3 x 3 - 3" grid pattern - no border necessary

4 x 4 - 4" grid pattern - no border necessary

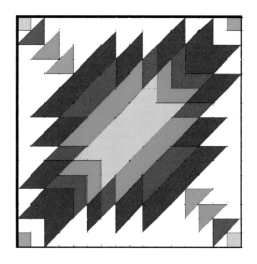 

Indian Spirit

Intermediate

16 Grid

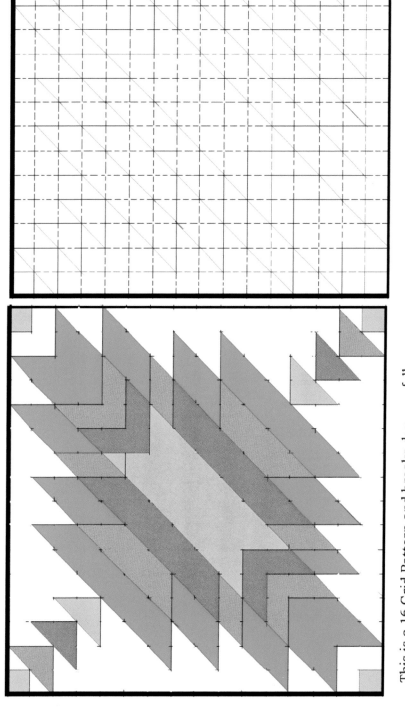

This is a 16 Grid Pattern and breaks down as follows:

It is recommended to place a border around this pattern for ease if you cannot divide evenly by 16.

2 x 2 - 1.5" grid pattern - no border necessary

3 x 3 - 2.25 grid pattern - no border necessary

4 x 4 - 3" grid pattern - no border necessary

161

e

"Art washes away from the soul the dust of everyday life."

— Pablo Picasso

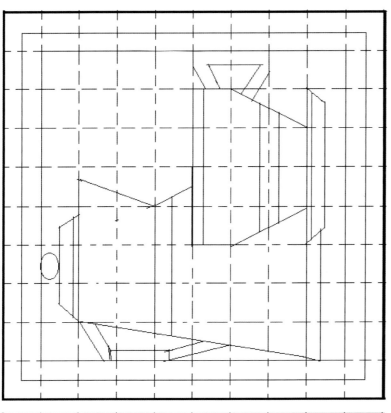

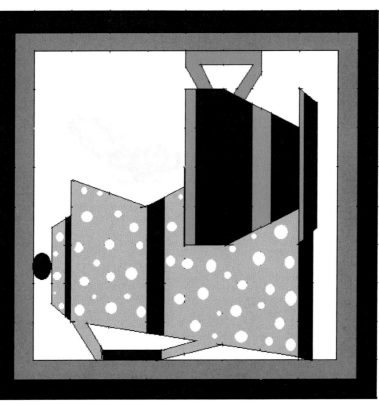

This is a 10 Grid Pattern and breaks down as follows:

It is recommended to place a border around this pattern for ease if you cannot divide evenly by 10.

2 x 2 - 2.25" grid pattern - .75" border necessary

3 x 3 - 3.5" grid pattern - .50" border necessary

4 x 4 - 4.75" grid pattern - slight border necessary

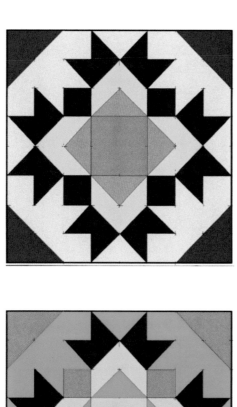

This pattern is an 8 Grid Pattern and breaks down as follows:

It is recommended to place a border around this pattern for ease if you cannot divide evenly by 8.

2 x 2 - 3" grid - no border necessary

3 x 3 - 4.5" grid - no border necessary

4 x 4 - 6" grid - no border necessary

166

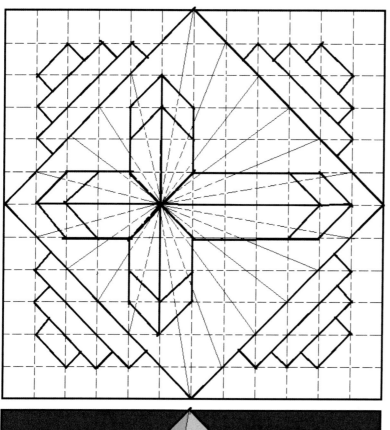

This is a 12 Grid Pattern and breaks down as follows:

It is recommended to place a border around this pattern for ease if you cannot divide evenly by 12.

2 x 2 - 2" grid pattern - no border necessary

3 x 3 - 3" grid pattern - no border necessary

4 x 4 - 4" grid pattern - no border necessary

Lily   Intermediate   12 Grid

This is a 12 Grid Pattern and breaks down as follows:

It is recommended to place a border around this pattern for ease if you cannot divide evenly by 12.

2 x 2 - 2" grid pattern - no border necessary

3 x 3 - 3" grid pattern - no border necessary

4 x 4 - 4" grid pattern - no border necessary

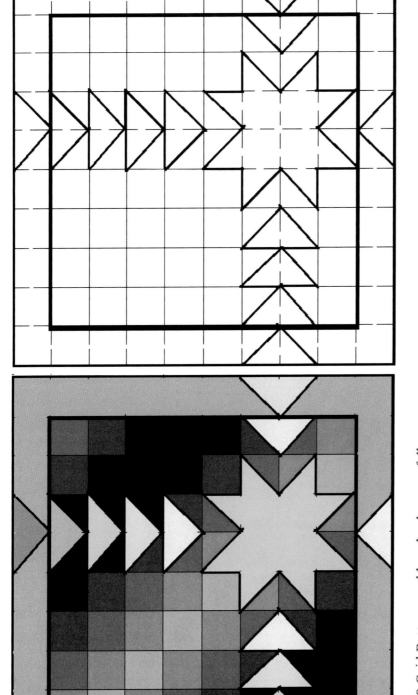

This is a 10 Grid Pattern and breaks down as follows:

It is recommended to place a border around this pattern for ease if you cannot divide evenly by 10.

2 x 2 - 2.25" grid pattern - .75" border necessary

3 x 3 - 3.5" grid pattern - .50" border necessary

4 x 4 - 4.75" grid pattern - slight border necessary

This is a 16 Grid Pattern and breaks down as follows:

It is recommeded to place a border around this pattern for ease if you cannot divide evenly by 16.

2 x 2 - 1.5" grid pattern - no border necessary

3 x 3 - 2.25 grid pattern - no border necessary

4 x 4 - 3" grid pattern - no border necessary

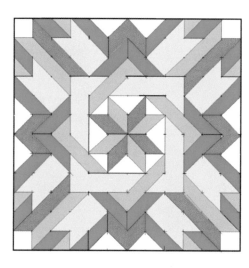

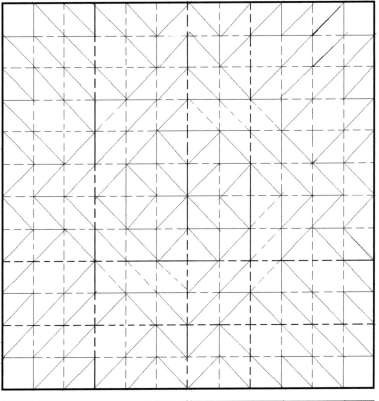

This is a 12 Grid Pattern and breaks down as follows:

It is recommended to place a border around this pattern for ease if you cannot divide evenly by 12.

2 x 2 - 2" grid pattern - no border necessary

3 x 3 - 3" grid pattern - no border necessary

4 x 4 - 4" grid pattern - no border necessary

176

Love Note   Intermediate   6 Grid

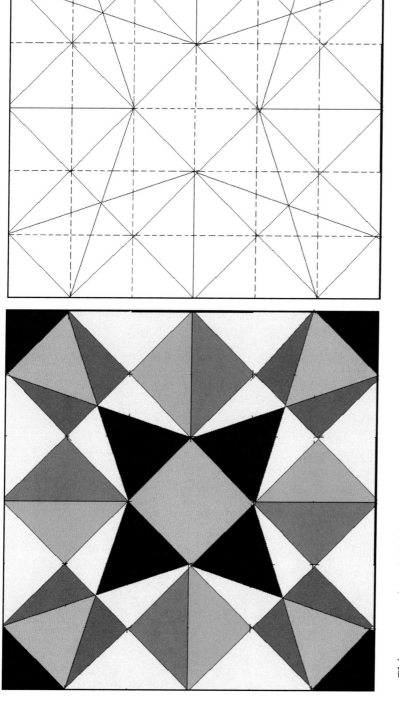

This pattern is a 6 Grid Pattern and breaks down as follows:

It is recommended to place a border around this pattern for ease if you cannot divide evenly by 6.

2 x 2 - 4" grid - no border necessary

3 x 3 - 6" grid - no border necessary

4 x 4 - 8" grid - no border necessary

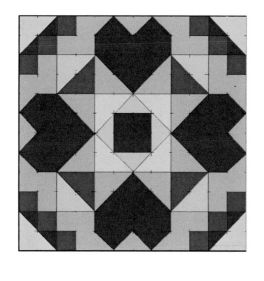

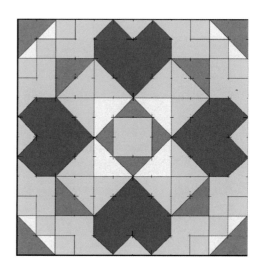

Loving Hearts   Intermediate   12 Grid

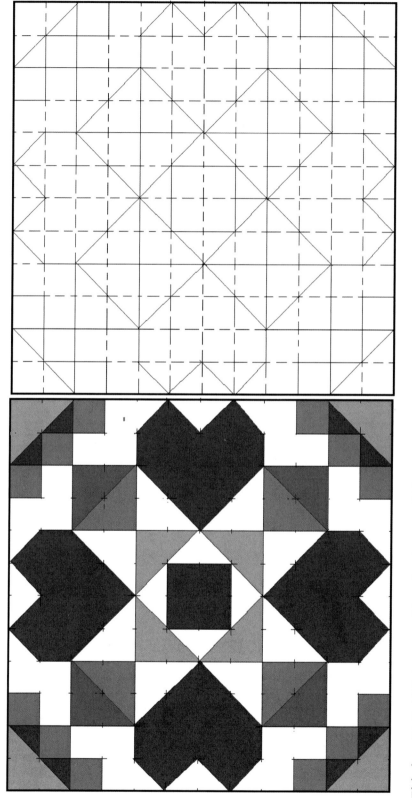

This is a 12 Grid Pattern and breaks down as follows:

It is recommended to place a border around this pattern for ease if you cannot divide evenly by 12.

2 x 2 - 2" grid pattern - no border necessary

3 x 3 - 3" grid pattern - no border necessary

4 x 4 - 4" grid pattern - no border necessary

 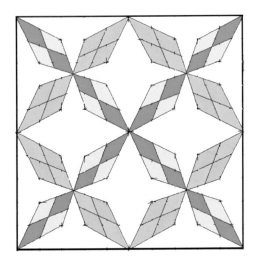

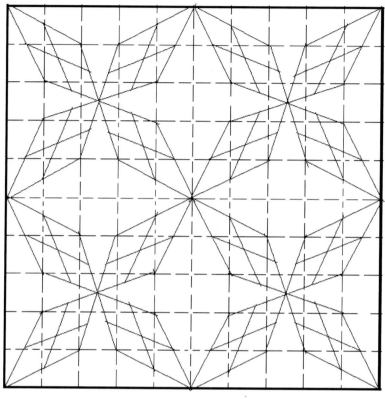

This is a 10 Grid Pattern and breaks down as follows:

It is recommended to place a border around this pattern for ease if you cannot divide evenly by 10.

2 x 2 - 2.25" grid pattern - .75" border necessary

3 x 3 - 3.5" grid pattern - .50" border necessary

4 x 4 - 4.75" grid pattern - slight border necessary

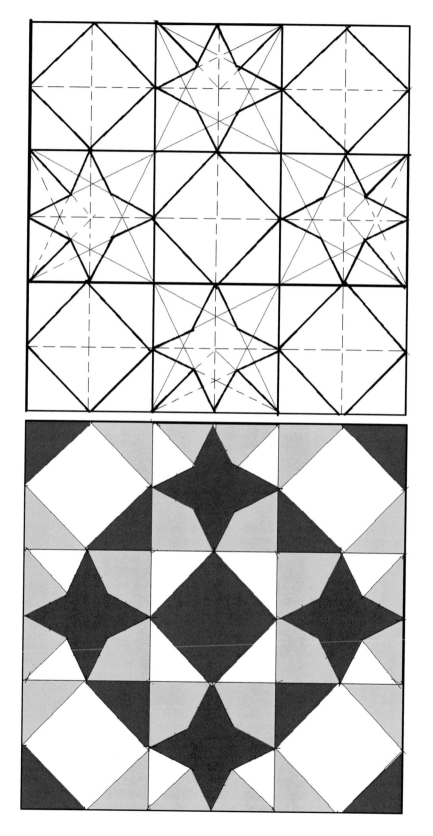

Tip: Remember those red lines show where to lay your straight edge to get you connecting points and lines.

This pattern is a 6 Grid Pattern and breaks down as follows:

It is recommended to place a border around this pattern for ease if you cannot divide evenly by 6.

2 x 2 - 4" grid - no border necessary

3 x 3 - 6" grid - no border necessary

4 x 4 - 8" grid - no border necessary

 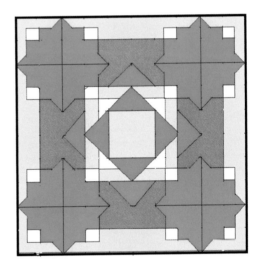

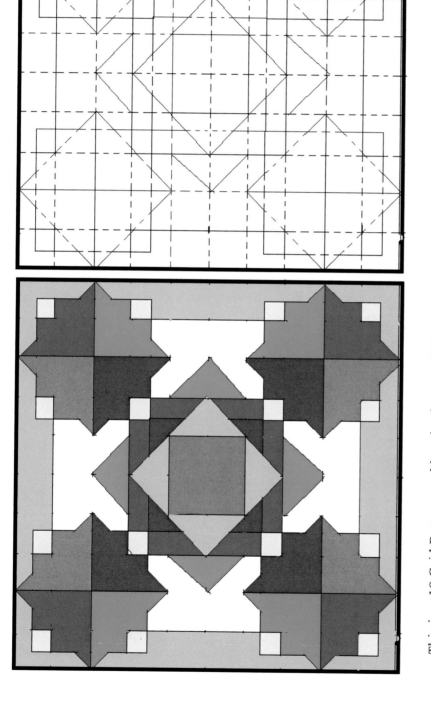

This is a 10 Grid Pattern and breaks down as follows:

It is recommended to place a border around this pattern for ease if you cannot divide evenly by 10.

2 x 2 - 2.25" grid pattern - .75" border necessary

3 x 3 - 3.5" grid pattern - .50" border necessary

4 x 4 - 4.75" grid pattern - slight border necessary

e

"Have no fear of perfection, you'll never reach it." — Salvador Dali

Paradise   Intermediate   10 Grid

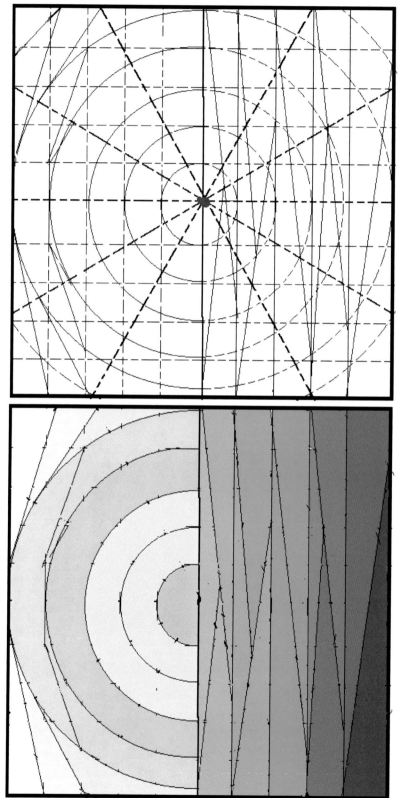

This is a 10 Grid Pattern and breaks down as follows:

It is recommended to place a border around this pattern for ease if you cannot divide evenly by 10.

2 x 2 - 2.25" grid pattern - .75" border necessary

3 x 3 - 3.5" grid pattern - .50" border necessary

4 x 4 - 4.75" grid pattern - slight border necessary

This pattern is an 8 Grid Pattern and breaks down as follows:

It is recommended to place a border around this pattern for ease if you cannot divide evenly by 8.

2 x 2 - 3" grid - no border necessary

3 x 3 - 4.5" grid - no border necessary

4 x 4 - 6" grid - no border necessary

Patchwork Ribbon   Intermediate   12 Grid

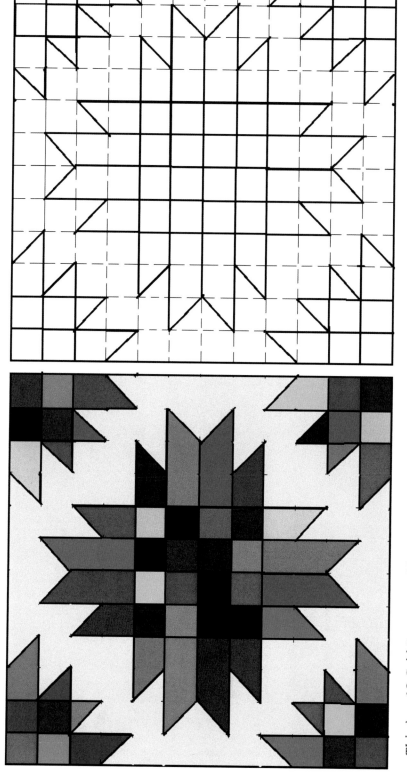

This is a 12 Grid Pattern and breaks down as follows:

It is recommended to place a border around this pattern for ease if you cannot divide evenly by 12.

2 x 2 - 2" grid pattern - no border necessary

3 x 3 - 3" grid pattern - no border necessary

4 x 4 - 4" grid pattern - no border necessary

Pearl Appeal Intermediate 8 Grid

This pattern is an 8 Grid Pattern and breaks down as follows:

It is recommended to place a border around this pattern for ease if you cannot divide evenly by 8.

2 x 2 - 3" grid - no border necessary

3 x 3 - 4.5" grid - no border necessary

4 x 4 - 6" grid - no border necessary

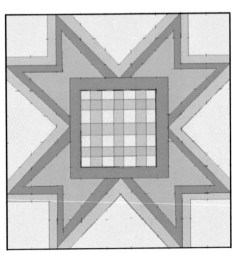

194

This pattern is a 9 Grid Pattern and breaks down as follows:

It is recommended to place a border around this pattern for ease if you cannot divide evenly by 9.

2 x 2 - 2.5" grid pattern - border necessary

3 x 3 - 4" grid pattern - no border necessary

4 x 4 - 5.25" grid pattern - border necessary

This is a 12 Grid Pattern and breaks down as follows:

It is recommended to place a border around this pattern for ease if you cannot divide evenly by 12.

2 x 2 - 2" grid pattern - no border necessary

3 x 3 - 3" grid pattern - no border necessary

4 x 4 - 4" grid pattern - no border necessary

Plaid Star   Intermediate   8 Grid

This pattern is an 8 Grid Pattern and breaks down as follows:

It is recommended to place a border around this pattern for ease if you cannot divide evenly by 8.

2 x 2 - 3" grid - no border necessary

3 x 3 - 4.5" grid - no border necessary

4 x 4 - 6" grid - no border necessary

This pattern is an 8 Grid Pattern and breaks down as follows:

It is recommended to place a border around this pattern for ease if you cannot divide evenly by 8.

2 x 2 - 3" grid - no border necessary

3 x 3 - 4.5" grid - no border necessary

4 x 4 - 6" grid - no border necessary

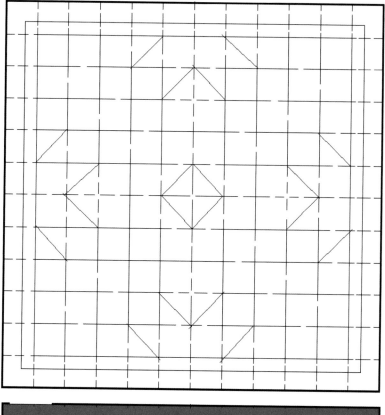

This is a 12 Grid Pattern and breaks down as follows:

It is recommended to place a border around this pattern for ease if you cannot divide evenly by 12.

2 x 2 - 2" grid pattern - no border necessary

3 x 3 - 3" grid pattern - no border necessary

4 x 4 - 4" grid pattern - no border necessary

This is a 12 Grid Pattern and breaks down as follows:

It is recommended to place a border around this pattern for ease if you cannot divide evenly by 12.

2 x 2 - 2" grid pattern - no border necessary

3 x 3 - 3" grid pattern - no border necessary

4 x 4 - 4" grid pattern - no border necessary

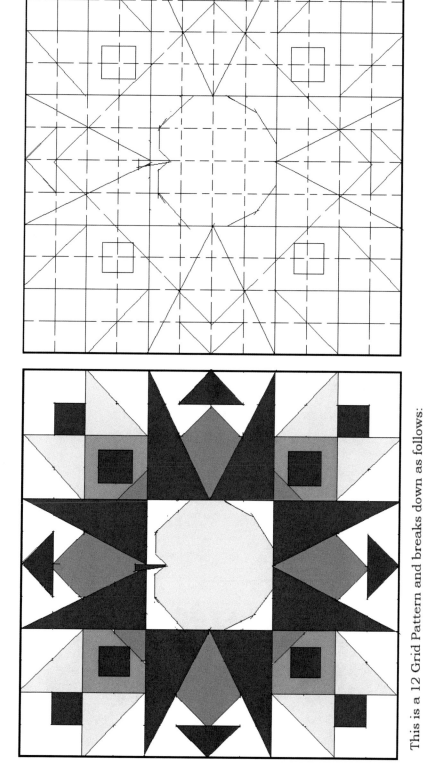

Tip: This image is shown with an apple in the center but you could ad any image such as an initial, silhouette, or logo.

This is a 12 Grid Pattern and breaks down as follows:

It is recommended to place a border around this pattern for ease if you cannot divide evenly by 12.

2 x 2 - 2" grid pattern - no border necessary

3 x 3 - 3" grid pattern - no border necessary

4 x 4 - 4" grid pattern - no border necessary

208

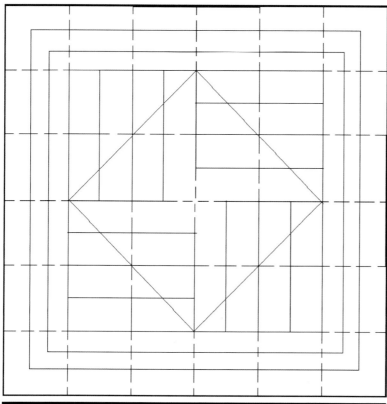

This pattern is a 6 Grid Pattern and breaks down as follows:

It is recommended to place a border around this pattern for ease if you cannot divide evenly by 6.

2 x 2 - 4" grid - no border necessary

3 x 3 - 6" grid - no border necessary

4 x 4 - 8" grid - no border necessary

e

"Every artist was first an amateur." – Ralph Waldo Emerson

Simple Snowflake   Beginner   16 Grid

This is a 16 Grid Pattern and breaks down as follows:

It is recommeded to place a border around this pattern for ease if you cannot divide evenly by 16.

2 x 2 - 1.5" grid pattern - no border necessary

3 x 3 - 2.25 grid pattern - no border necessary

4 x 4 - 3" grid pattern - no border necessary

This is a 12 Grid Pattern and breaks down as follows:

It is recommended to place a border around this pattern for ease if you cannot divide evenly by 12.

2 x 2 - 2" grid pattern - no border necessary

3 x 3 - 3" grid pattern - no border necessary

4 x 4 - 4" grid pattern - no border necessary

Summer Breeze   Intermediate   6 Grid

This pattern is a 6 Grid Pattern and breaks down as follows:

It is recommended to place a border around this pattern for ease if you cannot divide evenly by 6.

2 x 2 - 4" grid - no border necessary

3 x 3 - 6" grid - no border necessary

4 x 4 - 8" grid - no border necessary

Talara's Hummingbird   BQHO   Intermediate   12 Grid

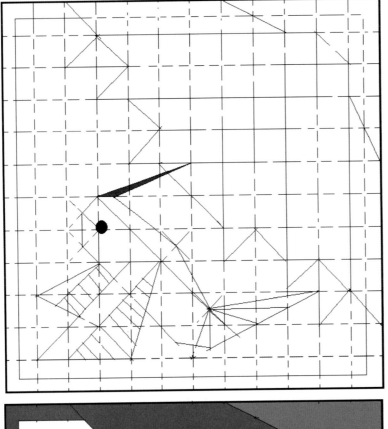

Tip: Use your imagination and break the flower down to add more colors and divisions.

This is a 12 Grid Pattern and breaks down as follows:

It is recommended to place a border around this pattern for ease if you cannot divide evenly by 12.

2 x 2 - 2" grid pattern - no border necessary

3 x 3 - 3" grid pattern - no border necessary

4 x 4 - 4" grid pattern - no border necessary

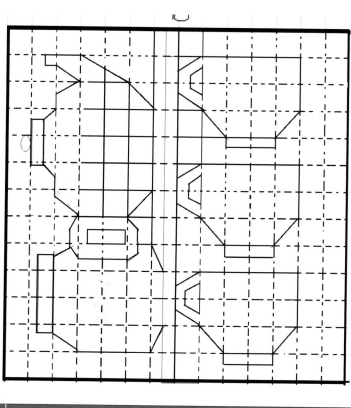

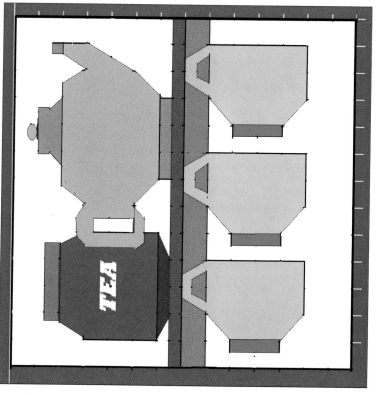

This is a 12 Grid Pattern and breaks down as follows:

It is recommended to place a border around this pattern for ease if you cannot divide evenly by 12.

2 x 2 - 2" grid pattern - no border necessary

3 x 3 - 3" grid pattern - no border necessary

4 x 4 - 4" grid pattern - no border necessary

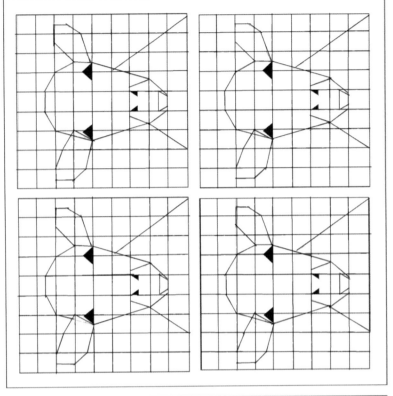

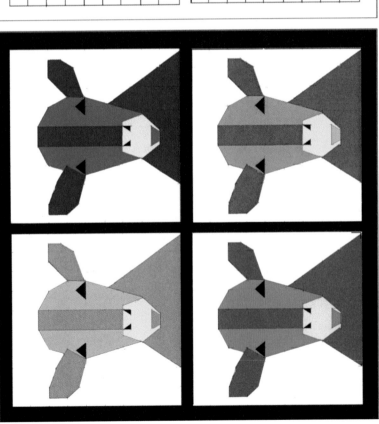

This pattern is broken into four quads with framing around each of those.

The grid with the quad is 9 grid.

A 2 x 2 – Grid is 1″, the frame is 2″ evenly around each quad.

A 3 x 3 – Grid is 1 5/8, the center frame is 2″ – measure from the center out and the remaining makes the outside frame.

A 4 x 4 – Grid is 2.25, the frame is 2.5″ evenly around each quad.

This is a 10 Grid Pattern and breaks down as follows:

It is recommended to place a border around this pattern for ease if you cannot divide evenly by 10.

2 x 2 - 2.25" grid pattern - .75" border necessary

3 x 3 - 3.5" grid pattern - .50" border necessary

4 x 4 - 4.75" grid pattern - slight border necessary

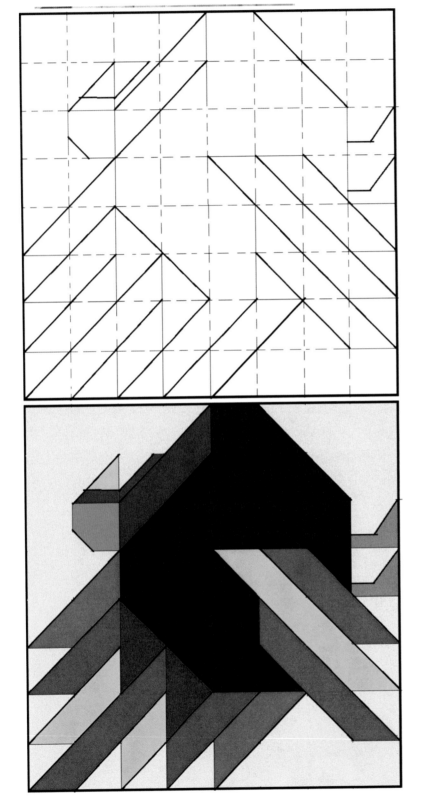

This pattern is an 8 Grid Pattern and breaks down as follows:

It is recommended to place a border around this pattern for ease if you cannot divide evenly by 8.

2 x 2 - 3" grid - no border necessary

3 x 3 - 4.5" grid - no border necessary

4 x 4 - 6" grid - no border necessary

Tweet, Tweet   Intermediate   15 Grid

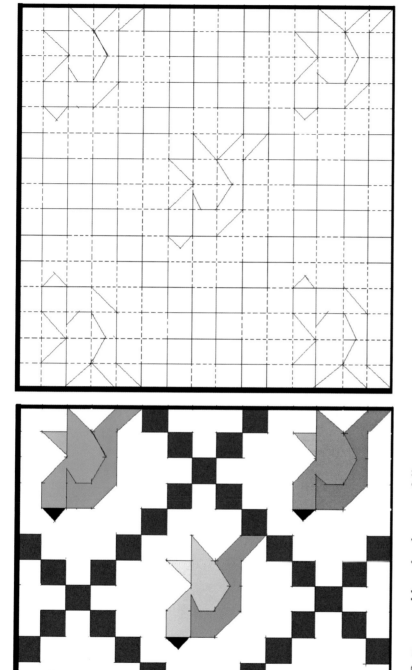

This is a 15 Grid Pattern and breaks down as follows:

It is recommended to place a border around this pattern for ease if you cannot divide evenly by 15

2 x 2 - 1.5" grid pattern - .75" border necessary

3 x 3 - 2.25" grid pattern - 1" border necessary

4 x 4 - 3" grid pattern - 1.5" border necessary

This pattern is an 8 Grid Pattern and breaks down as follows:

It is recommended to place a border around this pattern for ease if you cannot divide evenly by 8.

2 x 2 - 3" grid - no border necessary

3 x 3 - 4.5" grid - no border necessary

4 x 4 - 6" grid - no border necessary

Weavers Braid   Intermediate   9 Grid

This pattern is a 9 Grid Pattern and breaks down as follows:

It is recommended to place a border around this pattern for ease if you cannot divide evenly by 9.

2 x 2 - 2.5" grid pattern - border necessary

3 x 3 - 4" grid pattern - no border necessary

4 x 4 - 5.25" grid pattern - border necessary

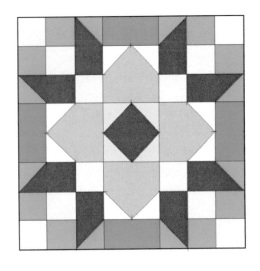

Wildflower   BQHO   Intermediate   8 Grid

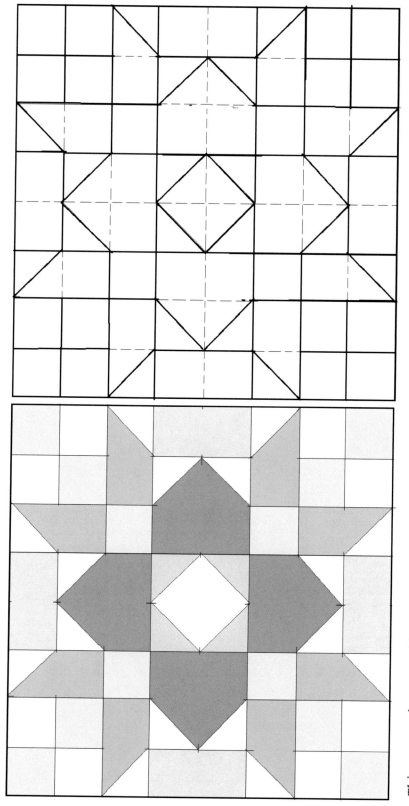

This pattern is an 8 Grid Pattern and breaks down as follows:

It is recommended to place a border around this pattern for ease if you cannot divide evenly by 8.

2 x 2 - 3" grid - no border necessary

3 x 3 - 4.5" grid - no border necessary

4 x 4 - 6" grid - no border necessary

This is a 16 Grid Pattern and breaks down as follows:

It is recommeded to place a border around this pattern for ease if you cannot divide evenly by 16.

2 x 2 - 1.5" grid pattern – no border necessary

3 x 3 - 2.25 grid pattern - no border necessary

4 x 4 - 3" grid pattern - no border necessary

 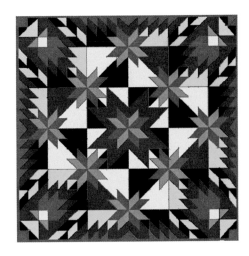

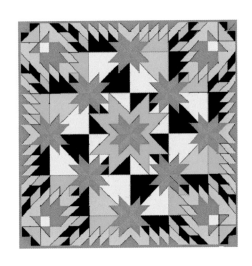 

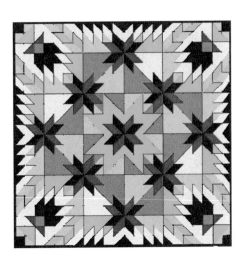 

This is a 22 Grid Pattern and breaks down as follows:

It is recommended to place a border around this pattern for ease if you cannot divide evenly by 22.

2 x 2 – 1" grid pattern – border necessary

3 x 3 – 1.50" grid pattern – border necessary

4 x 4 – 2" grid pattern – border necessary

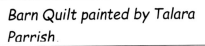

Barn Quilt painted by Talara Parrish.

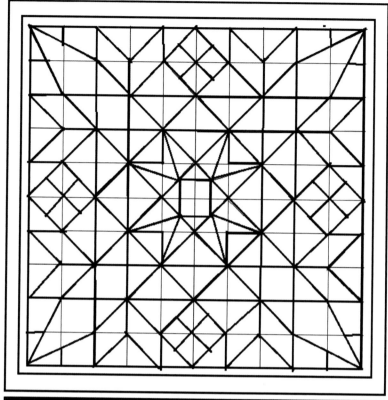

This is a 12 Grid Pattern and breaks down as follows:

It is recommended to place a border around this pattern for ease if you cannot divide evenly by 12.

2 x 2 - 2" grid pattern - no border necessary

3 x 3 - 3" grid pattern - no border necessary

4 x 4 - 4" grid pattern - no border necessary

This is a 12 Grid Pattern and breaks down as follows:

It is recommended to place a border around this pattern for ease if you cannot divide evenly by 12.

2 x 2 - 2" grid pattern - no border necessary

3 x 3 - 3" grid pattern - no border necessary

4 x 4 - 4" grid pattern - no border necessary

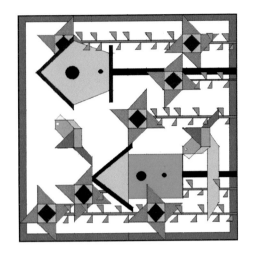 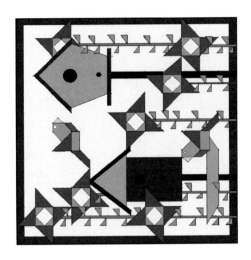

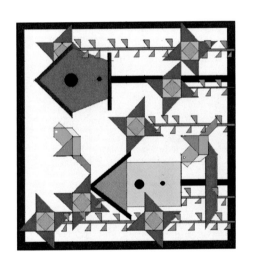 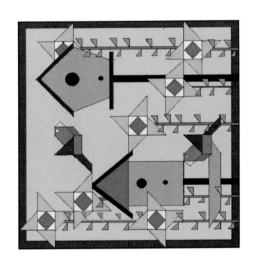

 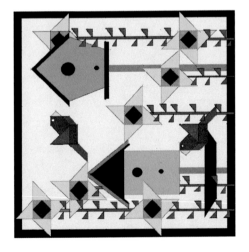

Bird Watching   BQHO   Advance   12 Grid

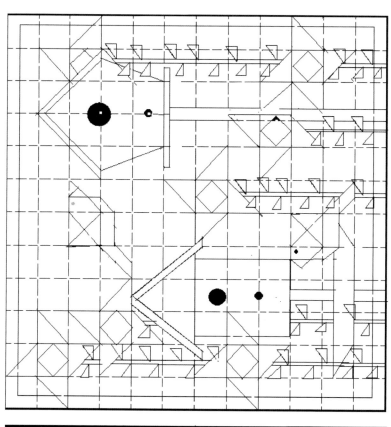

This is a 12 Grid Pattern and breaks down as follows:

It is recommended to place a border around this pattern for ease if you cannot divide evenly by 12.

2 x 2 - 2" grid pattern - no border necessary

3 x 3 - 3" grid pattern - no border necessary

4 x 4 - 4" grid pattern - no border necessary

This pattern is an 8 Grid Pattern and breaks down as follows:

It is recommended to place a border around this pattern for ease if you cannot divide evenly by 8.

2 x 2 - 3" grid - no border necessary

3 x 3 - 4.5" grid - no border necessary

4 x 4 - 6" grid - no border necessary

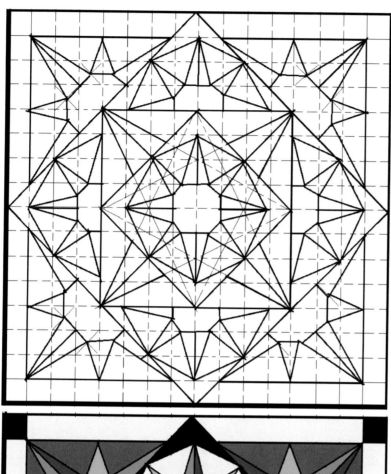

This is a 16 Grid Pattern and breaks down as follows:

It is recommeded to place a border around this pattern for ease if you cannot divide evenly by 16.

2 x 2 - 1.5" grid pattern - no border necessary

3 x 3 - 2.25 grid pattern - no border necessary

4 x 4 - 3" grid pattern - no border necessary

 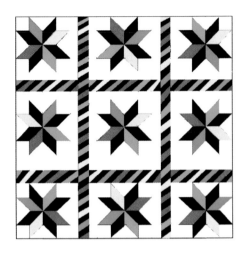

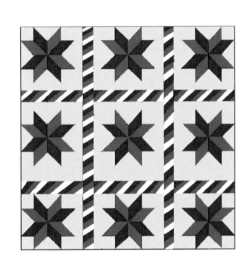 

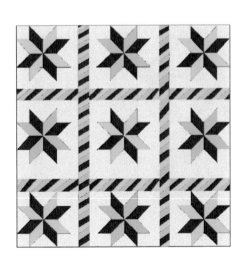 

This is a 16 Grid Pattern and breaks down as follows:

It is recommeded to place a border around this pattern for ease if you cannot divide evenly by 16.

2 x 2 - 1.5" grid pattern - no border necessary

3 x 3 - 2.25 grid pattern - no border necessary

4 x 4 - 3" grid pattern - no border necessary

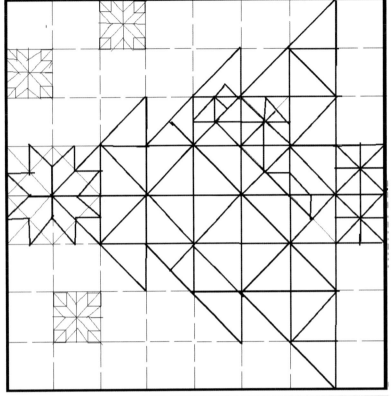

This pattern is an 8 Grid Pattern and breaks down as follows:

It is recommended to place a border around this pattern for ease if you cannot divide evenly by 8.

2 x 2 - 3" grid - no border necessary

3 x 3 - 4.5" grid - no border necessary

4 x 4 - 6" grid - no border necessary

e

"A good artist has less time than ideas." — Martin Kippenberger

 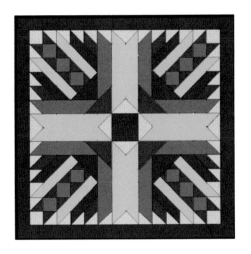

246

This is a 16 Grid Pattern and breaks down as follows:

It is recommeded to place a border around this pattern for ease if you cannot divide evenly by 16.

2 x 2 - 1.5" grid pattern - no border necessary

3 x 3 - 2.25 grid pattern - no border necessary

4 x 4 - 3" grid pattern - no border necessary

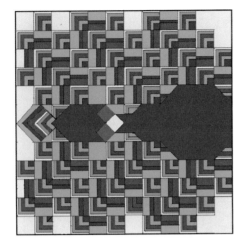
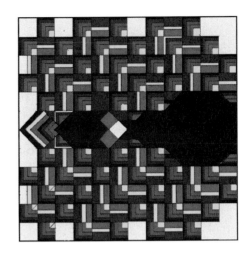
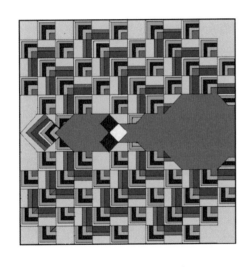
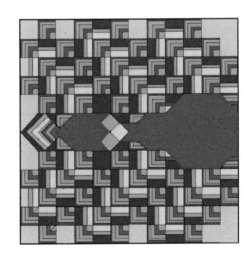

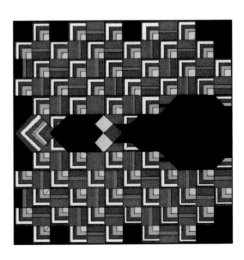

248

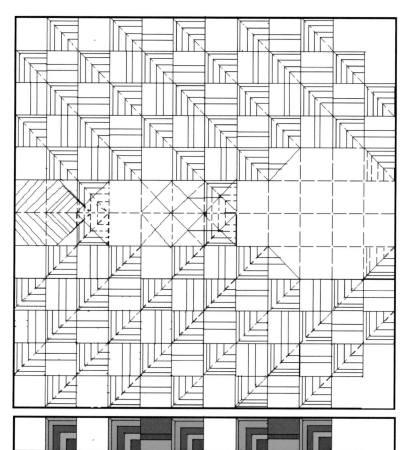

This is a 12 Grid Pattern and breaks down as follows:

It is recommended to place a border around this pattern for ease if you cannot divide evenly by 12.

2 x 2 - 2" grid pattern - no border necessary

3 x 3 - 3" grid pattern - no border necessary

4 x 4 - 4" grid pattern - no border necessary

Tip: There is no rule on breaking down the measurements to get the colors for feathers. Use your best judgement,

250

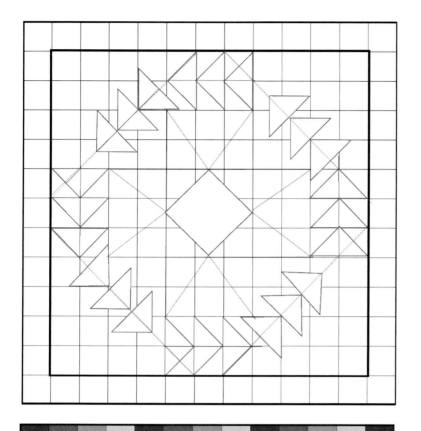

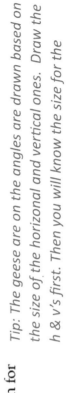

Tip: The geese are on the angles are drawn based on the size of the horizonal and vertical ones. Draw the h & v's first. Then you will know the size for the three corner ones.

This is a 13 Grid Pattern and breaks down as follows:

It is recommended to place a border around this pattern for ease if you cannot divide evenly by 13.

2 x 2 – 1.75" grid pattern – border necessary

3 x 3 – 2.75" grid pattern – border necessary

4 x 4 – 3.5" grid pattern – border necessary

This is a 16 Grid Pattern and breaks down as follows:

It is recommended to place a border around this pattern for ease if you cannot divide evenly by 16.

2 x 2 - 1.5" grid pattern - no border necessary

3 x 3 - 2.25 grid pattern - no border necessary

4 x 4 - 3" grid pattern - no border necessary

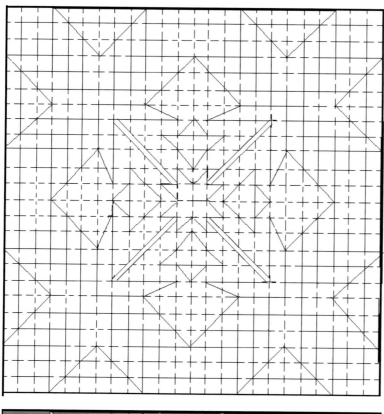

This is a 24 Grid Pattern and breaks down as follows:

It is recommended to place a border around this pattern for ease if you cannot divide evenly by 24.

2 x 2 - 1" grid pattern - no border necessary

3 x 3 - 1.5" grid pattern - no border necessary

4 x 4 - 2" grid pattern - no border necessary

This is a 24 Grid Pattern and breaks down as follows:

It is recommended to place a border around this pattern for ease if you cannot divide evenly by 24.

2 x 2 - 1" grid pattern - no border necessary

3 x 3 - 1.5" grid pattern - no border necessary

4 x 4 - 2" grid pattern - no border necessary

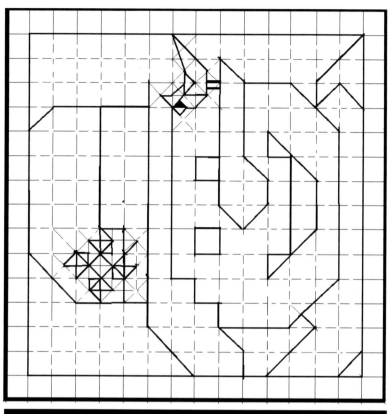

This is a 16 Grid Pattern and breaks down as follows:

It is recommeded to place a border around this pattern for ease if you cannot divide evenly by 16.

2 x 2 - 1.5" grid pattern - no border necessary

3 x 3 - 2.25 grid pattern - no border necessary

4 x 4 - 3" grid pattern - no border necessary

258

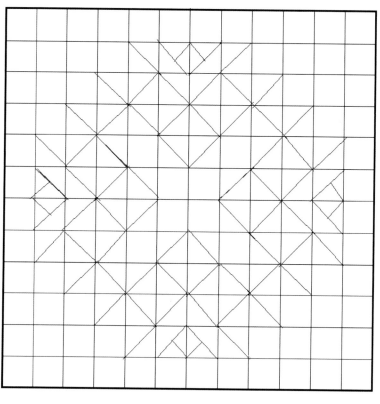

This is a 12 Grid Pattern and breaks down as follows:

It is recommended to place a border around this pattern for ease if you cannot divide evenly by 12.

2 x 2 - 2" grid pattern - no border necessary

3 x 3 - 3" grid pattern - no border necessary

4 x 4 - 4" grid pattern - no border necessary

e

An artist is not paid for his labor but for his vision.

&

— James McNeill Whistler

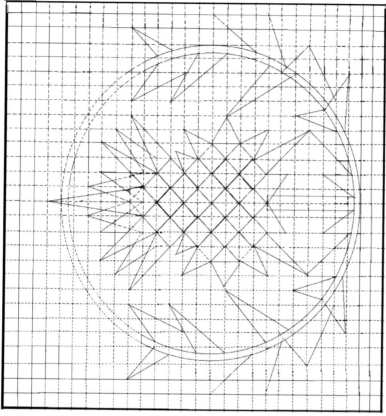

This pattern is a 28-grid pattern. Dotted lines show the grid and connecting points.

2 x 2 – Grid is 3/4" – remaining measurement is made part of outer border.

3 x 3 – Grid is 1 1/4" – remaining measurement is made part of outer border.

4 x 4 – Grid is 1 5/8" – remaining measurement is made part of outer border.

Begin measuring from the center edge out to mark the grid.

This is a 16 Grid Pattern and breaks down as follows:

It is recommeded to place a border around this pattern for ease if you cannot divide evenly by 16.

2 x 2 - 1.5" grid pattern - no border necessary

3 x 3 - 2.25 grid pattern - no border necessary

4 x 4 - 3" grid pattern - no border necessary

e

"The greater the artist, the greater the doubt. Perfect confidence is granted to the less talented as a consolation prize."

– Robert Hughes

Monarch   BQHO   Advance   12 Grid

This is a 12 Grid Pattern and breaks down as follows:

It is recommended to place a border around this pattern for ease if you cannot divide evenly by 12.

2 x 2 - 2" grid pattern - no border necessary

3 x 3 - 3" grid pattern - no border necessary

4 x 4 - 4" grid pattern - no border necessary

Painted by Talara Parrish and entered the Our State magazine in NC. One of 5 finalist in a statewide competition. The blues and tans represent the Blue Ridge mountains and the teal and aqua represents the Carolina coast.

This pattern is an 18 Grid Pattern and breaks down as follows:

It is recommended to place a border around this pattern for ease if you cannot divide evenly by 18.

2 x 2 - 1.25" grid pattern - border necessary

3 x 3 - 2" grid pattern - no border necessary

4 x 4 - 2.5 grid pattern - border necessary

267

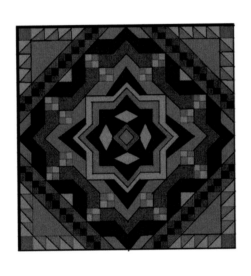 

268

Muse   BQHO   Advance   16 Grid

This is a 16 Grid Pattern and breaks down as follows:

It is recommeded to place a border around this pattern for ease if you cannot divide evenly by 16.

2 x 2 - 1.5" grid pattern - no border necessary

3 x 3 - 2.25 grid pattern - no border necessary

4 x 4 - 3" grid pattern - no border necessary

e

"Picasso had a saying – 'good artists copy, great artists steal' – and we have always been shameless about stealing great ideas."

— Walter Isaacson

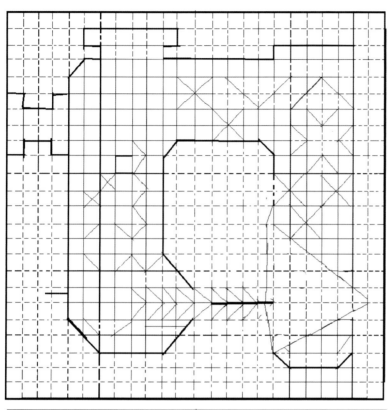

This is a 24 Grid Pattern and breaks down as follows:

It is recommended to place a border around this pattern for ease if you cannot divide evenly by 24.

2 x 2 - 1" grid pattern - no border necessary

3 x 3 - 1.5" grid pattern - no border necessary

4 x 4 - 2" grid pattern - no border necessary

This is a 12 Grid Pattern and breaks down as follows:

It is recommended to place a border around this pattern for ease if you cannot divide evenly by 12.

2 x 2 - 2" grid pattern - no border necessary

3 x 3 - 3" grid pattern - no border necessary

4 x 4 - 4" grid pattern - no border necessary

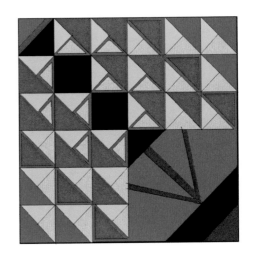

274

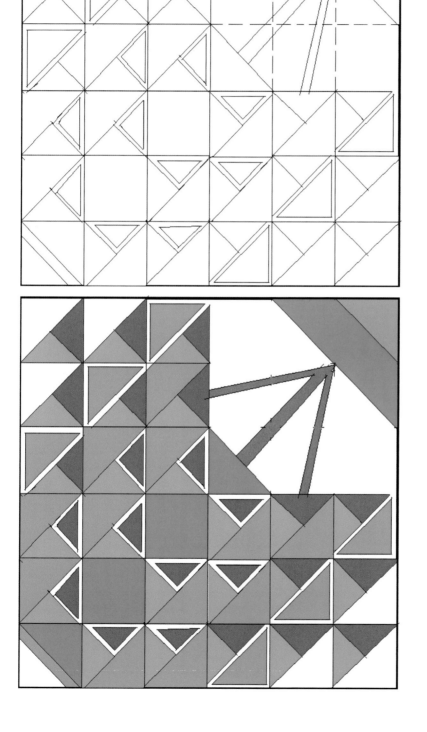

This pattern is a 6 Grid Pattern and breaks down as follows:

It is recommended to place a border around this pattern for ease if you cannot divide evenly by 6.

2 x 2 - 4" grid - no border necessary

3 x 3 - 6" grid - no border necessary

4 x 4 - 8" grid - no border necessary

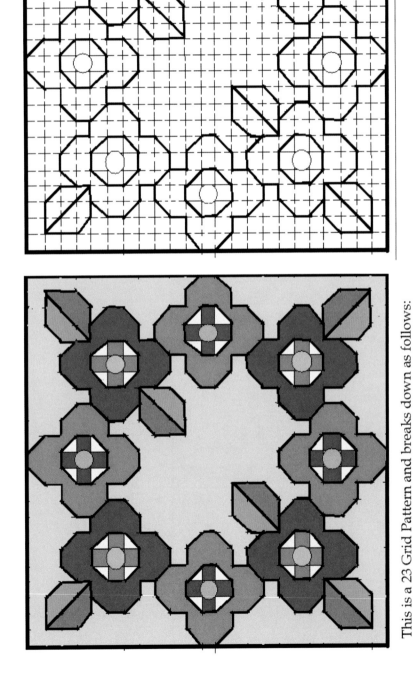

This is a 23 Grid Pattern and breaks down as follows:

It is recommended to place a border around this pattern for ease if you cannot divide evenly by 23.

2 x 2 – 1" grid pattern – border necessary

3 x 3 – 1.5: grid pattern – border necessary

4 x 4 – 2" grid pattern – border necessary

Tip: Start in the center and divide the grid in half to begin measurements. Amount remaining after marking grid size, is the border.

e

"I would rather be an artist than a leader. Ironically, a leader must follow the rules."

― Criss Jami

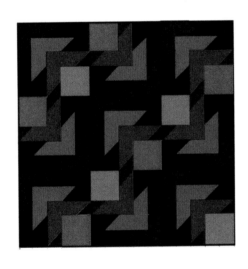 

278

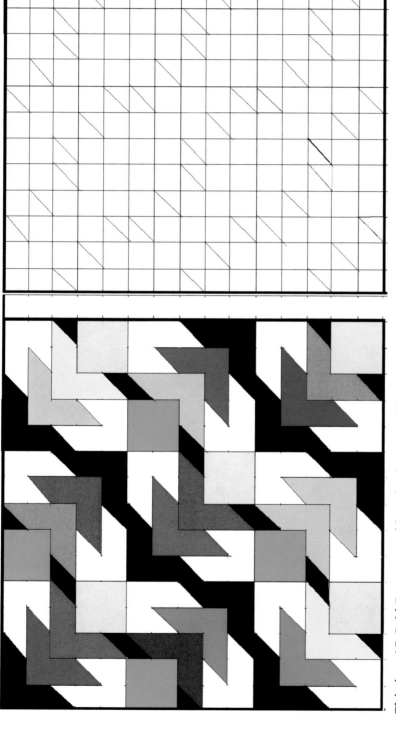

This is a 15 Grid Pattern and breaks down as follows:

It is recommended to place a border around this pattern for ease if you cannot divide evenly by 15

2 x 2 - 1.5" grid pattern - .75" border necessary

3 x 3 - 2.25" grid pattern - 1" border necessary

4 x 4 - 3" grid pattern - 1.5" border necessary

Phoenix   BQHO   Advance   16 Grid

This is a 16 Grid Pattern and breaks down as follows:

It is recommeded to place a border around this pattern for ease if you cannot divide evenly by 16.

2 x 2 - 1.5" grid pattern - no border necessary

3 x 3 - 2.25 grid pattern - no border necessary

4 x 4 - 3" grid pattern - no border necessary

This pattern is an 8 Grid Pattern and breaks down as follows:

It is recommended to place a border around this pattern for ease if you cannot divide evenly by 8.

2 x 2 - 3" grid - no border necessary

3 x 3 - 4.5" grid - no border necessary

4 x 4 - 6" grid - no border necessary

e

"The worst enemy to creativity is self-doubt." — Sylvia Plath

This is a 16 Grid Pattern and breaks down as follows:

It is recommeded to place a border around this pattern for ease if you cannot divide evenly by 16.

2 x 2 - 1.5" grid pattern - no border necessary

3 x 3 - 2.25 grid pattern - no border necessary

4 x 4 - 3" grid pattern - no border necessary

286

Rose Garden   BQHO   Advance   16 Grid

This is a 16 Grid Pattern and breaks down as follows:

It is recommeded to place a border around this pattern for ease if you cannot divide evenly by 16.

2 x 2 - 1.5" grid pattern - no border necessary

3 x 3 - 2.25 grid pattern - no border necessary

4 x 4 - 3" grid pattern - no border necessary

287

288

This is a 16 Grid Pattern and breaks down as follows:

It is recommeded to place a border around this pattern for ease if you cannot divide evenly by 16.

2 x 2 - 1.5" grid pattern - no border necessary

3 x 3 - 2.25 grid pattern - no border necessary

4 x 4 - 3" grid pattern - no border necessary

This is a 16 Grid Pattern and breaks down as follows:

It is recommeded to place a border around this pattern for ease if you cannot divide evenly by 16.

2 x 2 - 1.5" grid pattern - no border necessary

3 x 3 - 2.25 grid pattern - no border necessary

4 x 4 - 3" grid pattern - no border necessary

This is a 12 Grid Pattern and breaks down as follows:

It is recommended to place a border around this pattern for ease if you cannot divide evenly by 12.

2 x 2 - 2" grid pattern - no border necessary

3 x 3 - 3" grid pattern - no border necessary

4 x 4 - 4" grid pattern - no border necessary

 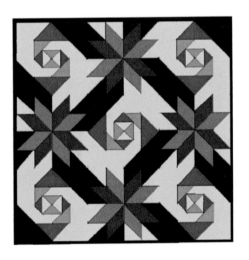

294

This is a 12 Grid Pattern and breaks down as follows:

It is recommended to place a border around this pattern for ease if you cannot divide evenly by 12.

2 x 2 - 2" grid pattern - no border necessary

3 x 3 - 3" grid pattern - no border necessary

4 x 4 - 4" grid pattern - no border necessary

This pattern is a 20 Grid Pattern and breaks down as follows:

It is recommended to place a border around this pattern for ease if you cannot divide evenly by 20.

2 x 2 - 1.13 (1 1/8") grid pattern - See Tip

3 x 3 - 1.75" grid pattern - See Tip

4 x 4 - 2.25" grid pattern - no border necessary

298

This is a 16 Grid Pattern and breaks down as follows:

It is recommeded to place a border around this pattern for ease if you cannot divide evenly by 16.

2 x 2 - 1.5" grid pattern - no border necessary

3 x 3 - 2.25 grid pattern - no border necessary

4 x 4 - 3" grid pattern - no border necessary

This is a 16 Grid Pattern and breaks down as follows:

It is recommended to place a border around this pattern for ease if you cannot divide evenly by 16.

2 x 2 - 1.5" grid pattern - no border necessary

3 x 3 - 2.25 grid pattern - no border necessary

4 x 4 - 3" grid pattern - no border necessary

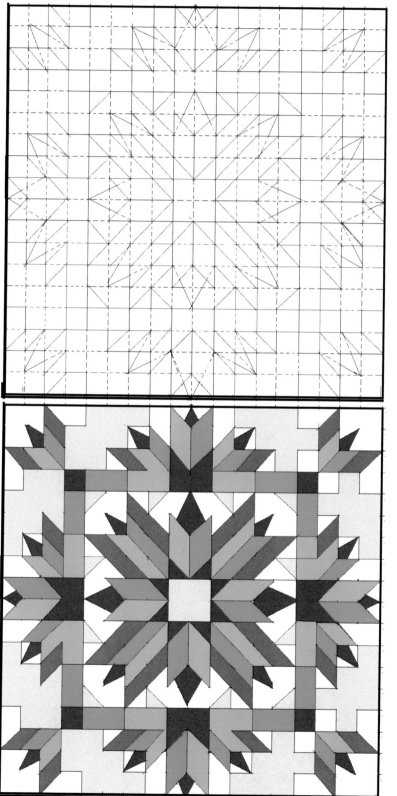

This pattern is an 18 Grid Pattern and breaks down as follows:

It is recommended to place a border around this pattern for ease if you cannot divide evenly by 18.

2 x 2 - 1.25" grid pattern - border necessary

3 x 3 - 2" grid pattern - no border necessary

4 x 4 - 2.5 grid pattern - border necessary

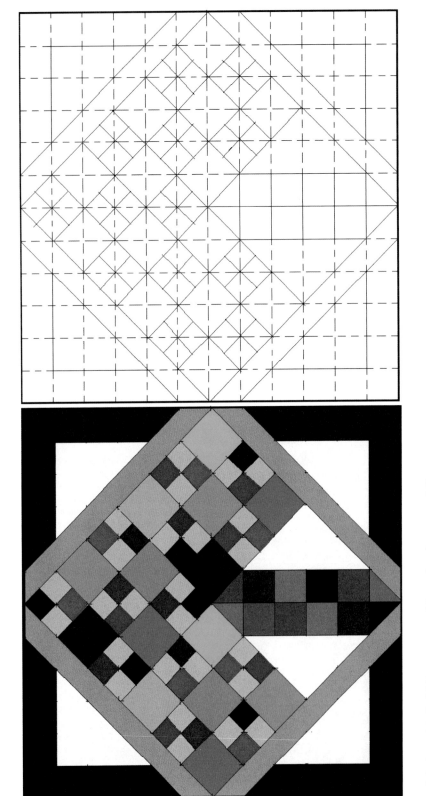

This is a 12 Grid Pattern and breaks down as follows:

It is recommended to place a border around this pattern for ease if you cannot divide evenly by 12.

2 x 2 - 2" grid pattern - no border necessary

3 x 3 - 3" grid pattern - no border necessary

4 x 4 - 4" grid pattern - no border necessary

This pattern is an 8 Grid Pattern and breaks down as follows:

It is recommended to place a border around this pattern for ease if you cannot divide evenly by 8.

2 x 2 - 3" grid - no border necessary

3 x 3 - 4.5" grid - no border necessary

4 x 4 - 6" grid - no border necessary

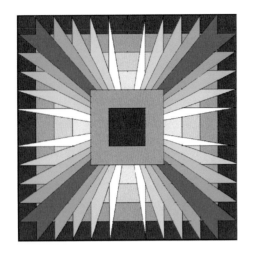 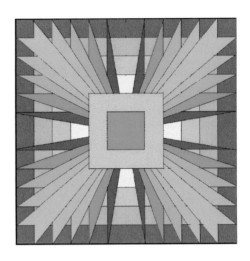

 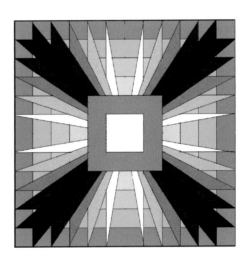

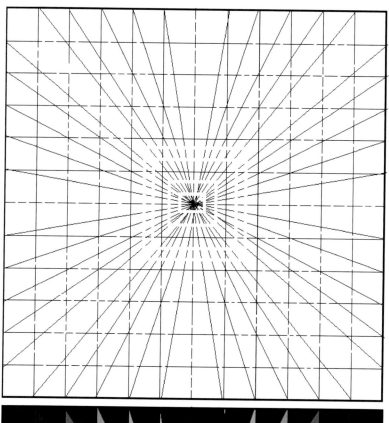

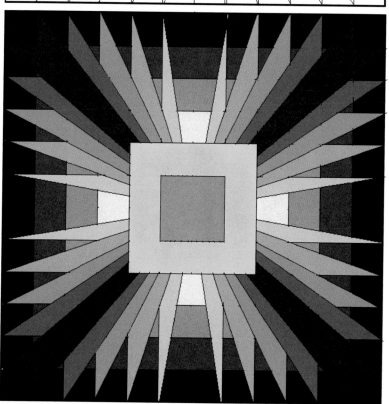

This is a 12 Grid Pattern and breaks down as follows:

It is recommended to place a border around this pattern for ease if you cannot divide evenly by 12.

2 x 2 - 2" grid pattern - no border necessary

3 x 3 - 3" grid pattern - no border necessary

4 x 4 - 4" grid pattern - no border necessary

e

"Anxiety is the handmaiden of creativity" — T. S. Eliot

Waving Flag   Advance   12 Grid

This is a 12 Grid Pattern and breaks down as follows:

It is recommended to place a border around this pattern for ease if you cannot divide evenly by 12.

2 x 2 - 2" grid pattern - no border necessary

3 x 3 - 3" grid pattern - no border necessary

4 x 4 - 4" grid pattern - no border necessary

Wildflower Seeds   Advance   24 Grid

This is a 24 Grid Pattern and breaks down as follows:

It is recommended to place a border around this pattern for ease if you cannot divide evenly by 24.

2 x 2 - 1" grid pattern - no border necessary

3 x 3 - 1.5" grid pattern - no border necessary

4 x 4 - 2" grid pattern - no border necessary

312

Measurements are out from the center of the pattern on the degrees.
Subtract the width of a border if a border is desired.

2 x 2 – Outer points at 12" from the center.

3 x 3 – Outer points at 18" from the center.

4 x 4 – Outer points at 24" from the center.

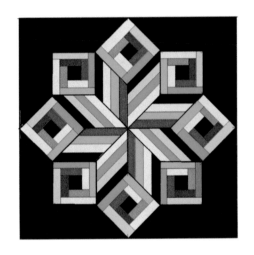

Birthday Surprise   Point Based   45 Degrees

Start by drawing lines at 45 degrees.

Connect the lateral points to the vertical points on the centers as shown in upper left.

Draw lines at 22.5 degrees out to lines just drawn as shown in upper left.

Connect points to center line as shown in upper left.

Erase lines as shown in upper right, finish corner squares out.

Divide sections by the number of colors desired for each section as shown in lower left.

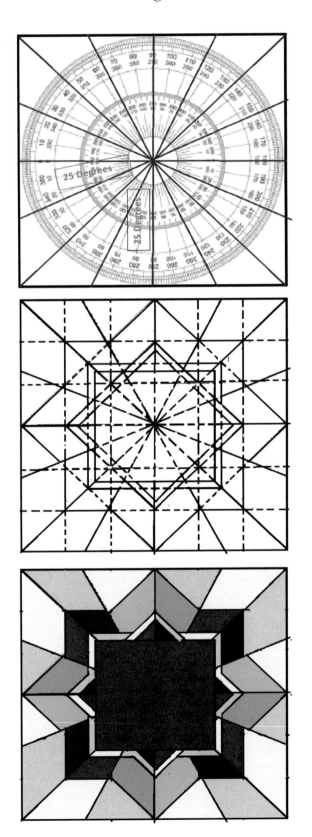

This patten is both point based, and grid based.

First, divide the width of the surface by 6 to get your grid size.

2 x 2 – Grid size is 4"

3 x 3 – Grid size is 6"

4 x 4 – Grid size is 8"

Once grid is drawn, divisions are as follows:
90 degrees, 22.5 degrees, 45 degrees

316

Dresden Daisy   Point Based   15 Degrees

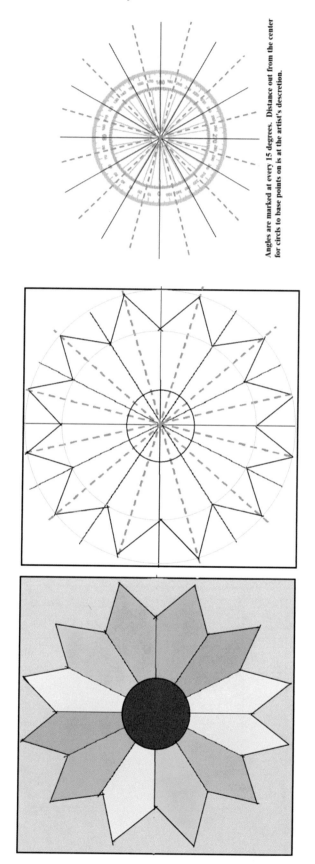

Angles are marked at every 15 degrees. Distance out from the center for circle to base points on is at the artist's descretion.

This pattern is based on a division of 15 degrees. Start by dividing the board into 4 grids. Then mark the degree lines within the outer circle. The come in from that circle the amount desired. The shorter the distance, the less sharp the points will be.

Fan Me   Point Based   15 Degrees

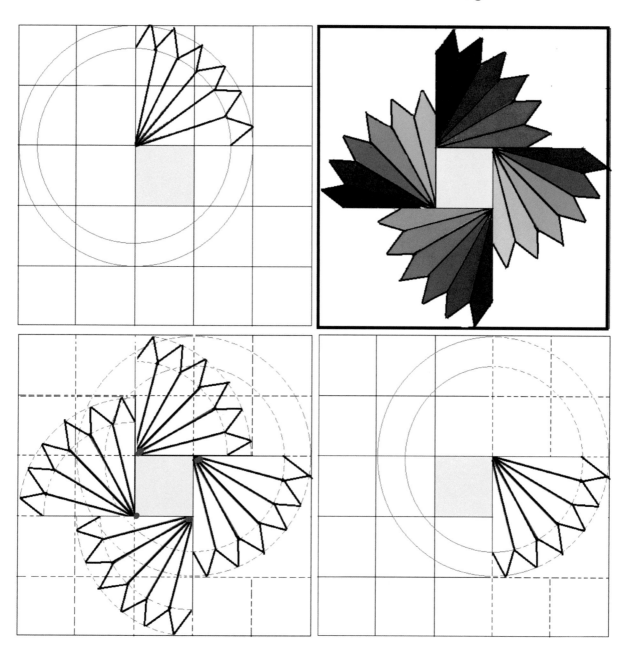

   This pattern is both a 5 Grid and point based. A border is necessary if you are unable to divide evenly by 5.

The red dots indicate the pivot point for the quarter circles. Make two at measurement desired.

Make lines at every 15 degrees in each quarter circle as shown to enter circle. Then connect points in center at outer circle to form points.

Fancy Mosaic Star   Point Based   20 Degrees

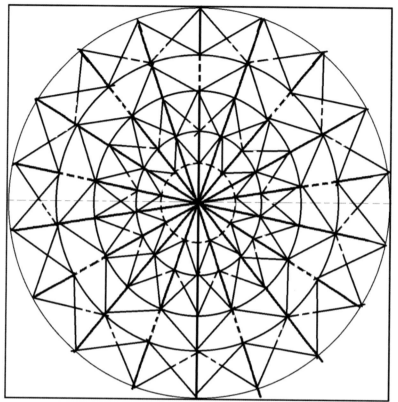

Draw 5 circles at equal distance apart or at a width desired.

Draw lines from edge to edge of circles at every 20 degrees.

Connect lines as shown to make points around the bands of the circle.

Erase any unnecessary lines.

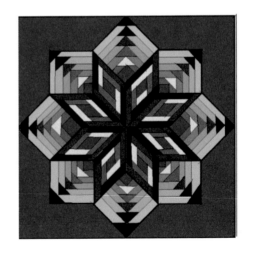

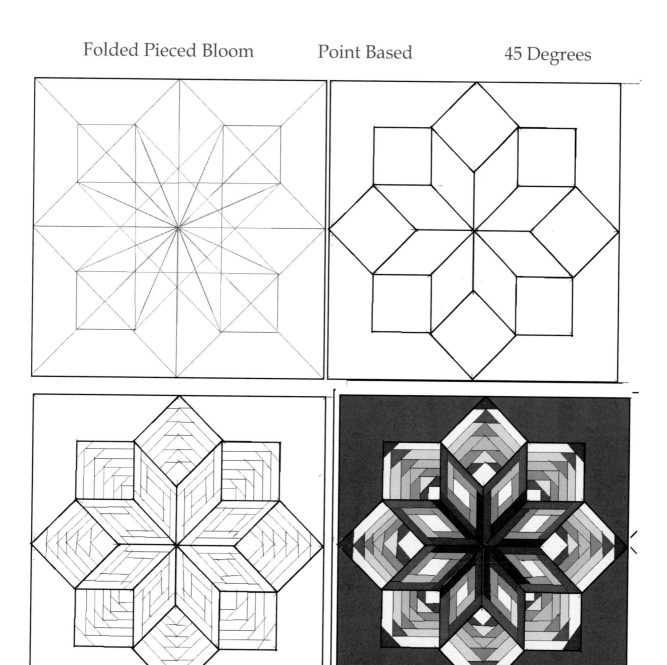

Folded Pieced Bloom   Point Based   45 Degrees

Start by drawing lines at 45 degrees.

Connect the lateral points to the vertical points on the centers as shown in upper left.

Draw lines at 22.5 degrees out to lines just drawn as shown in upper left.

Connect points to center line as shown in upper left.

Erase lines as shown in upper right, finish corner squares out.

Divide sections by the number of colors desired for each section as shown in lower left.

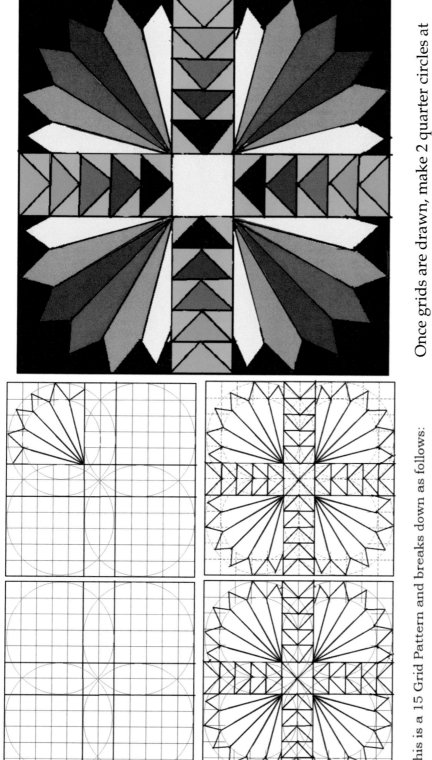

Once grids are drawn, make 2 quarter circles at pivot points at the distance desired. The make lines at every 15 degree to inner circle. Next connect points from inner circle to outer circle to form points.

This is a 15 Grid Pattern and breaks down as follows:

It is recommended to place a border around this pattern for ease if you cannot divide evenly by 15

2 x 2 - 1.5" grid pattern - .75" border necessary

3 x 3 - 2.25" grid pattern - 1" border necessary

4 x 4 - 3" grid pattern - 1.5" border necessary

Tip: Once you have drawn the basic pattern, then divide individual sections as desired to get the striping.

Measurements are out from the center of the pattern on the degrees.
Subtract the width of a border if a border is desired.

2 x 2 – Outer points at 12″ from the center.

3 x 3 – Outer points at 18″ from the center.

4 x 4 – Outer points at 24″ from the center.

328

Measurements are out from the center of the pattern on the degrees.
Subtract the width of a border if a border is desired.

2 x 2 - Outer points at 12″ from the center.

3 x 3 - Outer points at 18″ from the center.

4 x 4 - Outer points at 24″ from the center.

Measurements are out from the center of the pattern on the degrees. Subtract the width of a border if a border is desired.

2 x 2 - Outer points at 12" from the center.

3 x 3 – Outer points at 18" from the center.

4 x 4 – Outer points at 24" from the center.

Tip: Take the measurement of the 22.5 degree line and divide by two. This gives the first two connecting points shown in red. That distance is where your connecting point for the 3rd connecting point on the 45 degrees. For instance, on a 12" the point would be at 6" on the 22.5 line. Make line across and the space between the two green marks in what you make the 3rd point shown in

332

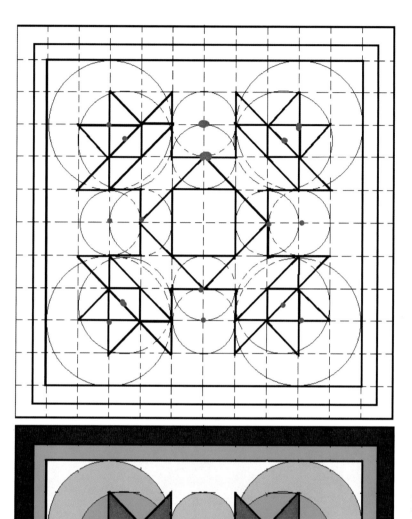

Red dot marks pivot point.

This is a 12 Grid Pattern and breaks down as follows:

It is recommended to place a border around this pattern for ease if you cannot divide evenly by 12.

2 x 2 - 2" grid pattern - no border necessary

3 x 3 - 3" grid pattern - no border necessary

4 x 4 - 4" grid pattern - no border necessary

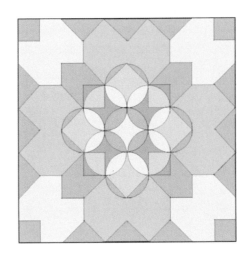

Blessed Cathedral   BQHO   Circle Based   10 Grid

This pattern is a 6 Grid Pattern and breaks down as follows:

It is recommended to place a border around this pattern for ease if you cannot divide evenly by 6.

2 x 2 - 4" grid - no border necessary

3 x 3 - 6" grid - no border necessary

4 x 4 - 8" grid - no border necessary

e

"All forms of madness, bizarre habits, awkwardness in society, general clumsiness, are justified in the person who creates good art."

— Roman Payne

Bobble   BQHO   Circle Based   6 Grid

This pattern is a 6 Grid Pattern and breaks down as follows:

It is recommended to place a border around this pattern for ease if you cannot divide evenly by 6.

2 x 2 - 4" grid - no border necessary

3 x 3 - 6" grid - no border necessary

4 x 4 - 8" grid - no border necessary

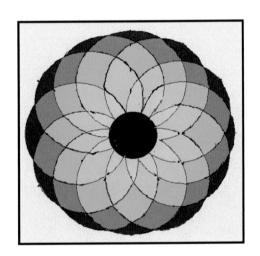
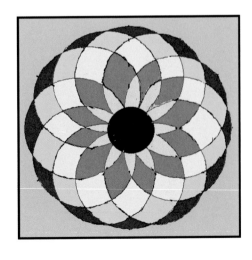
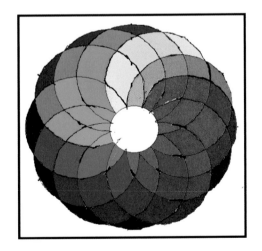

Dahlia Bloom   Point & Circle Based   30 Degrees

Mark your divisions at every 30 degrees for this pattern.

2 x 2 Outer points are at 12" (less border desired if any)

3 x 3 Outer points are at 18" (less border desired if any)

4 x 4Outer points are at 24" (less border desired if any)

The pivot point is half the line out for each circle.

339

Family Affair   BQHO   Circle Based   10 Grid

This is a 10 Grid Pattern and breaks down as follows:

It is recommended to place a border around this pattern for ease if you cannot divide evenly by 10.

2 x 2 - 2.25" grid pattern - .75" border necessary

3 x 3 - 3.5" grid pattern - .50" border necessary

4 x 4 - 4.75" grid pattern - slight border necessary

This pattern is an 8 Grid Pattern and breaks down as follows:

It is recommended to place a border around this pattern for ease if you cannot divide evenly by 8.

2 x 2 - 3" grid - no border necessary

3 x 3 - 4.5" grid - no border necessary

4 x 4 - 6" grid - no border necessary

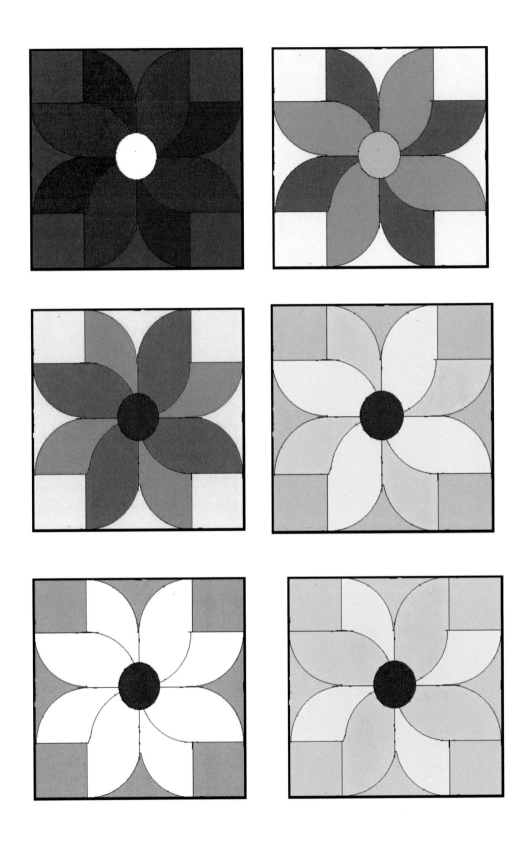

Glorious   Circle Based   4 Grid

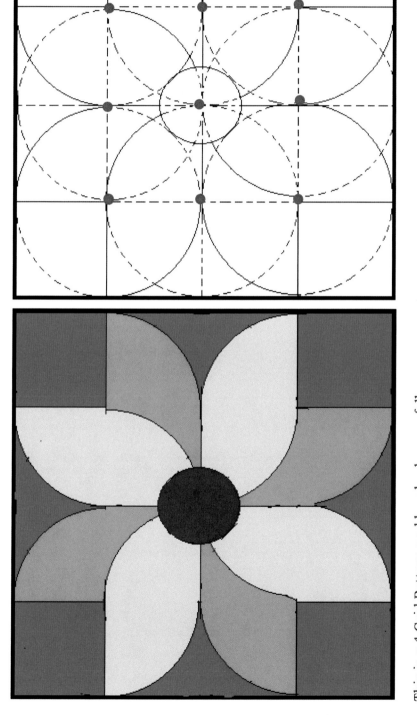

This is a 4 Grid Pattern and breaks down as follows:

It is recommended to place a border around this pattern for ease if you cannot divide evenly by 4.

2 x 2 - 6" grid pattern - no border necessary

3 x 3 - 9" grid pattern - no border necessary

4 x 4 - 12" grid pattern - no border necessary

Never Grow Up   Circle Based   4 Grid

This is a 4 Grid Pattern and breaks down as follows:

It is recommended to place a border around this pattern for ease if you cannot divide evenly by 4.

2 x 2 - 6" grid pattern - no border necessary

3 x 3 - 9" grid pattern - no border necessary

4 x 4 - 12" grid pattern - no border necessary

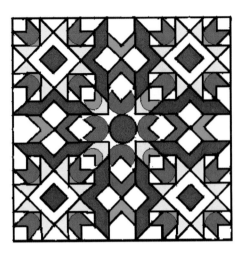

Prairie Dust   BQHO   Circle Based   16 Grid

This is a 16 Grid Pattern and breaks down as follows:

It is recommeded to place a border around this pattern for ease if you cannot divide evenly by 16.

2 x 2 - 1.5" grid pattern - no border necessary

3 x 3 - 2.25 grid pattern - no border necessary

4 x 4 - 3" grid pattern - no border necessary

349

350

This is a 7 Grid Pattern and breaks down as follows:

It is recommended to place a border around this pattern for ease if you cannot divide evenly by 7.

2 x 2 - 3.25" grid pattern - border necessary

3 x 3 - 5" grid pattern - border necessary

4 x 4 - 6.75 grid pattern - border necessary

352

This is a 12 Grid Pattern and breaks down as follows:

It is recommended to place a border around this pattern for ease if you cannot divide evenly by 12.

2 x 2 - 2" grid pattern - no border necessary

3 x 3 - 3" grid pattern - no border necessary

4 x 4 - 4" grid pattern - no border necessary

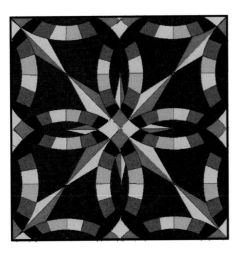

Tip: Once you draw the rings from the pivot point,
set the pivot point off the board so that you match
the points from center to edge to make outer rings
that are partially visible.

This is a 4 Grid Pattern and breaks down as follows:

It is recommended to place a border around this pattern for
ease if you cannot divide evenly by 4.

2 x 2 - 6" grid pattern - no border necessary

3 x 3 - 9" grid pattern - no border necessary

4 x 4 - 12" grid pattern - no border necessary

Additional Resources

Website: www.BarnQuiltHeadquarters.com

Facebook: barnquiltsnc

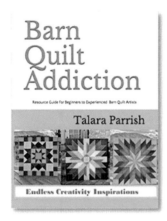 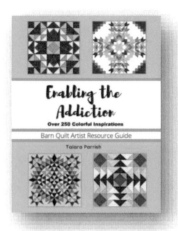

I want to personally invite you to join the blog! It is full of HOW-TO tutorial videos, tips and tricks that will save you money, time, and frustration. I also address common issues that subscribers inquire about along with tutorial videos on all kinds of patterns, techniques, problem solving and how to's.

www.barnquiltheadquarters.com/blog - click on any post to subscribe!

Check out ARTIST TOOLS on the menu for much more also.